St. Catharines Ontario Book 3 in Colour Photos, Saving Our History One Photo at a Time

Photography
by Barbara Raué
2018

Series Name:
Cruising Ontario

Book 191: St. Catharines Book 3

Cover photo: 343 Merritt Street, Page 44

Series Name: Cruising Ontario
Saving Our History One Photo at a Time
in colour photos

Books Available in Alphabetical Order:
Aberfoyle, Acton, Alton, Amherstburg, Ancaster, Arthur, Aylmer, Ayr, Bloomingdale, Brantford, Burlington, Caledon, Caledonia, Cambridge, Clifford, Conestogo, Delhi, Dorchester to Aylmer, Drayton, Drumbo, Dundas, Eden Mills, Elmira, Elora, Essex, Fergus, Guelph, Hagersville, Hamilton, Hanover, Harriston, Hespeler, Jarvis, Kingston, Kingsville, Kitchener, Linwood, Listowel, London, Lucknow, Mono, Mount Forest, Neustadt, New Hamburg, Niagara-on-the-Lake, Oakville, Orangeville, Orillia, Owen Sound, Palmerston, Peterborough, Petrolia, Port Elgin, Preston, Rockwood, Sarnia, Seaforth, Sheffield, Shelburne, Simcoe, Southampton, St. Jacobs, St. Marys, St. Thomas, Stoney Creek, Stratford, Thamesford, Tillsonburg, Waterdown, Waterford, Waterloo, Welland, Wellesley, Windsor, Wingham, Woodstock

Book 157: Brockville
Book 158: Merrickville
Book 159: Smiths Falls
Book 160: Portland, Newboro
Book 161: Westport & Area
Book 162: Perth
Book 163-166: Belleville
Book 167-168: Port Colborne
Book 169: Erin in Colour
Book 170: Goderich in Colour
Book 171: Sault Ste. Marie
Book 172: Lake Superior
Book 173-176: Thunder Bay
Book 177-179: Paris

Book 180: St. George
Book 182-183: Burford
Book 184: Mt Pleasant,
    Onondaga, Newport
Book 185-186: Grimsby
Book 187: Toronto in Colour
Book 188: Collingwood Colour
Book 189-193: St. Catharines

Other Books by Barbara Raue

Coins of Gold

Arrows, Indians and Love

The Life and Times of Barbara
Volume 1: Inventions That Have Enhanced My Life
Volume 2: Entertainment That I Have Enjoyed
Volume 3: East Coast Trips
Volume 4: Olympics Have Always Intrigued Me
Volume 5: Wonders of the World
Volume 6: Caribbean Cruises We Have Enjoyed
Volume 7: Animals
Volume 8: Storms and Other Major Disasters in My Lifetime
Volume 9: Wars, Terrorist Attacks and Major Disasters

The Cromwell Family Book

Laura Secord Discovered

Daddy Where Are You?

Montana Series
Book 1: Montana Dream
Book 2: Life on the Montana Frontier
Book 3: Montana to Boston and Back
Book 4: Montana Sons Go to War
Book 5: Montana Sons Return From War

Visit Barbara's website to view all of her books
http://barbararaue.ca

Table of Contents

Bayview Drive	Page 6
Christie Street	Page 25
Johnston Street	Page 29
St. Paul Crescent	Page 36
Bradley Street	Page 38
Mountain Street	Page 40
Merritt Street	Page 41
Chestnut Street East	Page 47
Moffatt Street	Page 48
Vine Street	Page 49
Rolls Avenue	Page 50
Architectural Terms	Page 52
Building Styles	Page 58

St. Catharines is the largest city in Canada's Niagara Region in Southern Ontario. It is 51 kilometers (32 miles) south of Toronto across Lake Ontario, and is 19 kilometers (12 miles) inland from the international boundary with the United States along the Niagara River. It is the northern entrance of the Welland Canal. St. Catharines carries the official nickname "The Garden City" due to its 1,000 acres of parks, gardens and trails. The city was first settled by Loyalists in the 1780s. The Crown granted them land in compensation for their services and for losses in the United States. Early histories credit Sergeant Jacob Dittrick and Private John Hainer, formerly of Butler's Rangers, as among the first to come to the area. They took their Crown Patents where Dick's Creek and 12 Mile Creek merge, now the city center of St. Catharines.

Secondary to water routes, native trails provided transportation networks, resulting in the present-day radial road pattern from the City center.

After the Butler's Rangers disbanded in 1784 and settled the area, Duncan Murray as a former Quartermaster was appointed by the Crown to distribute free Government supplies (victuals) for two years to the resettled Loyalists. He did this from his mill, built on the 12 Mile Creek in Power Glen. After his death in 1786, his holdings went to merchant Robert Hamilton of Queenston. Hamilton became land wealthy, expropriating lands from subsistence Loyalist settlers who were incapable of settling their debts. Hamilton's major profits were derived from transshipping supplies for the military and civic establishments from his Queenston enterprise. He sold his business to Jesse Thompson before the turn of the 18th century.

The Merritt family arrived; they were among the later Loyalists to relocate following the American Revolution. In 1796, Thomas Merritt arrived to build on his relationship with his former Commander and Queen's Ranger, John Graves Simcoe, now the Lieutenant Governor of Upper Canada.

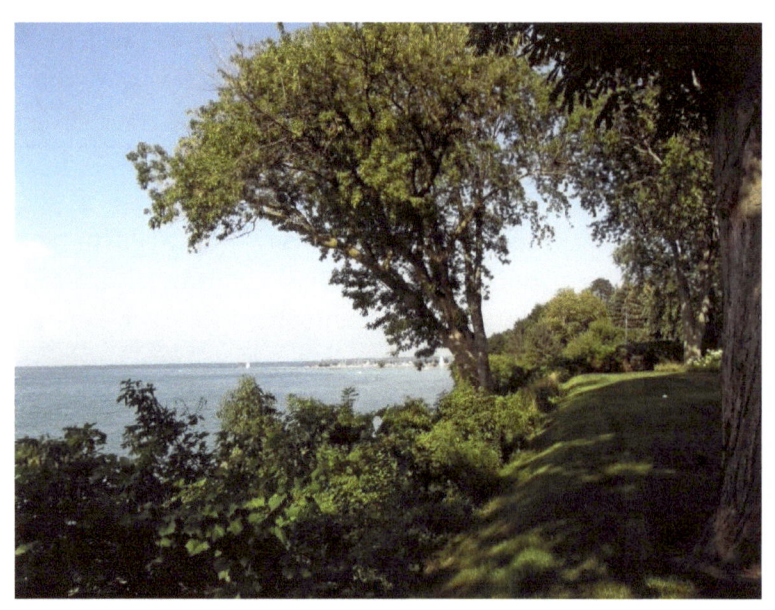

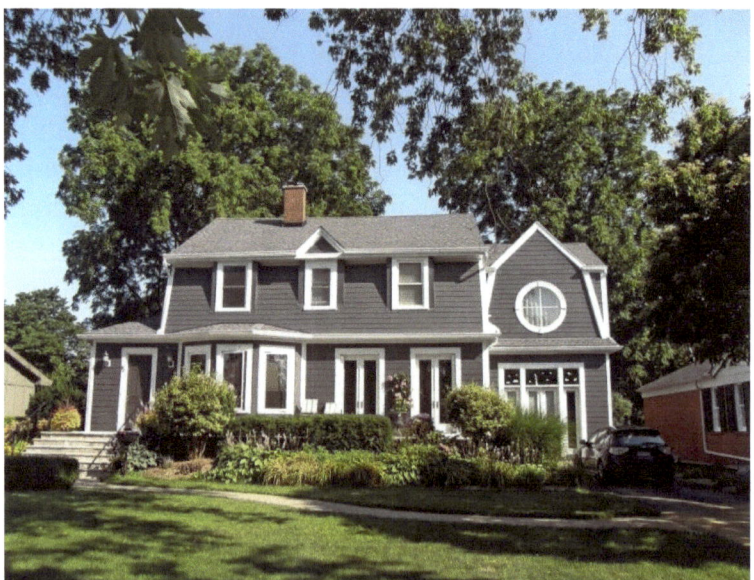

15 Bayview Drive

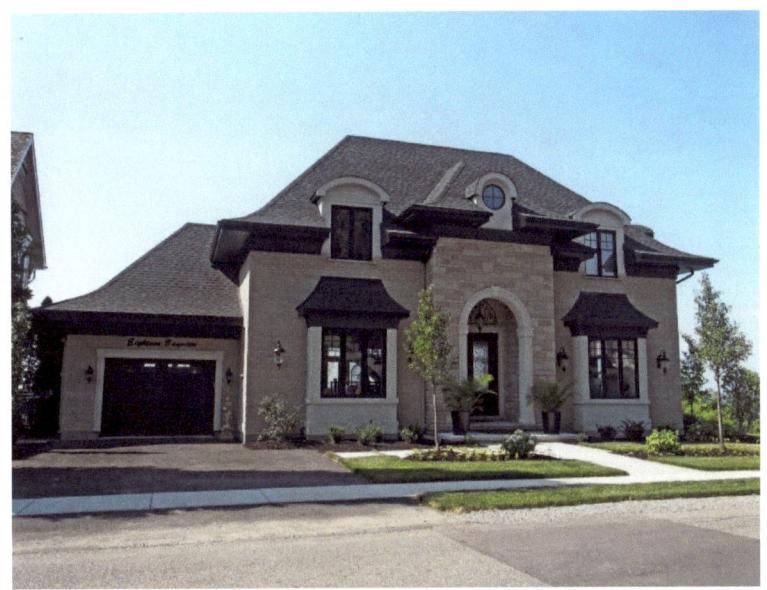

18 Bayview Drive – Mansard-type roof with dormers, bay windows with hoods

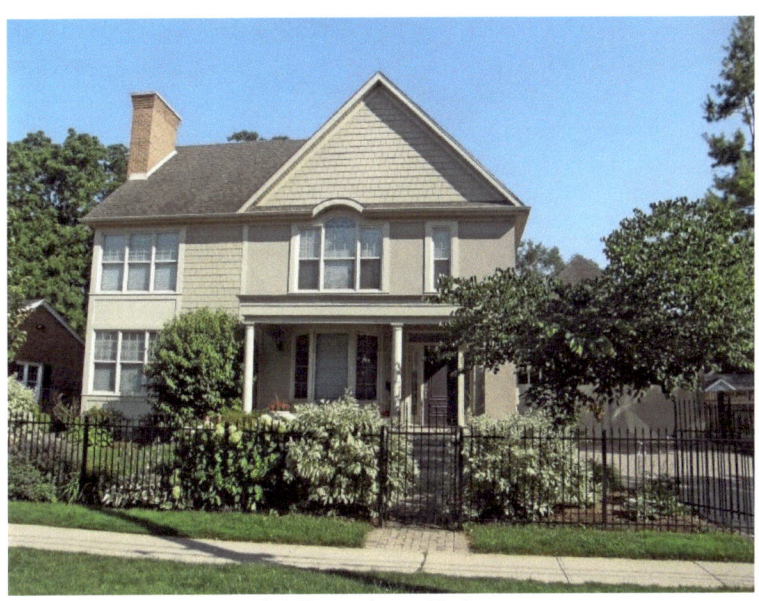

21 Bayview Drive

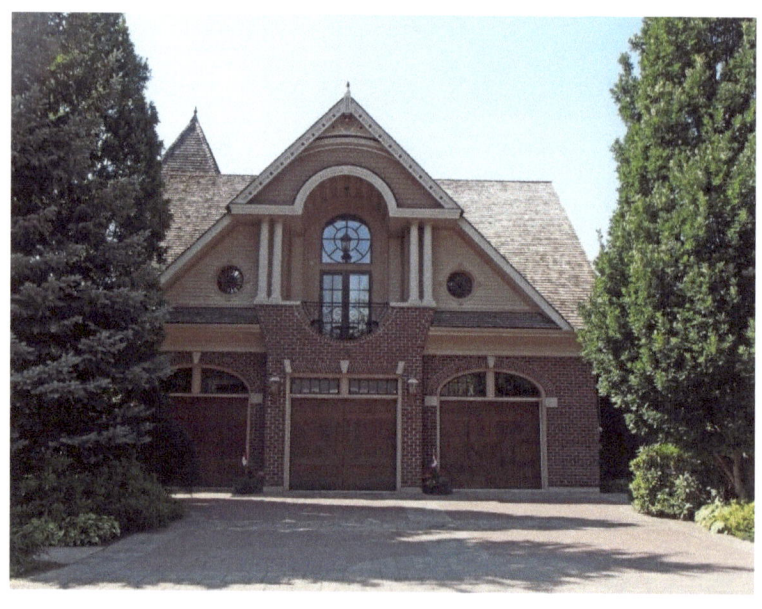

20 Bayview Drive – Doric pillars with open balcony above entrance

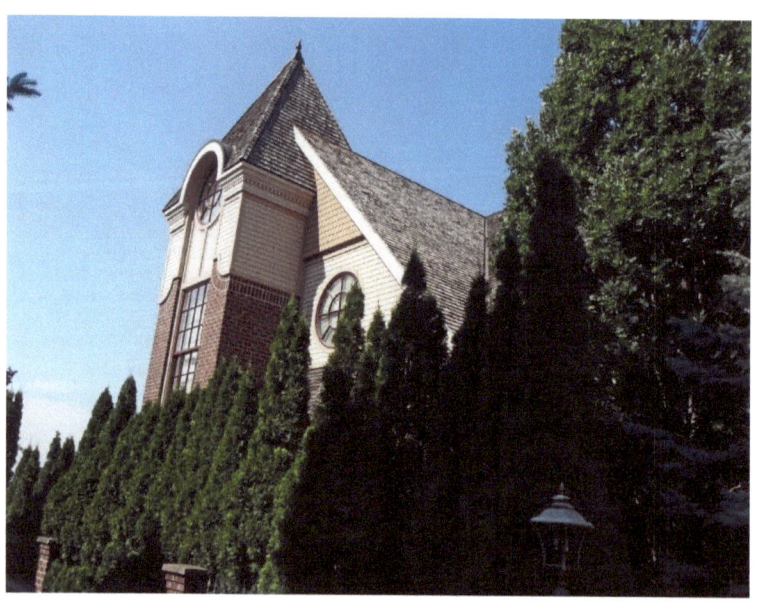

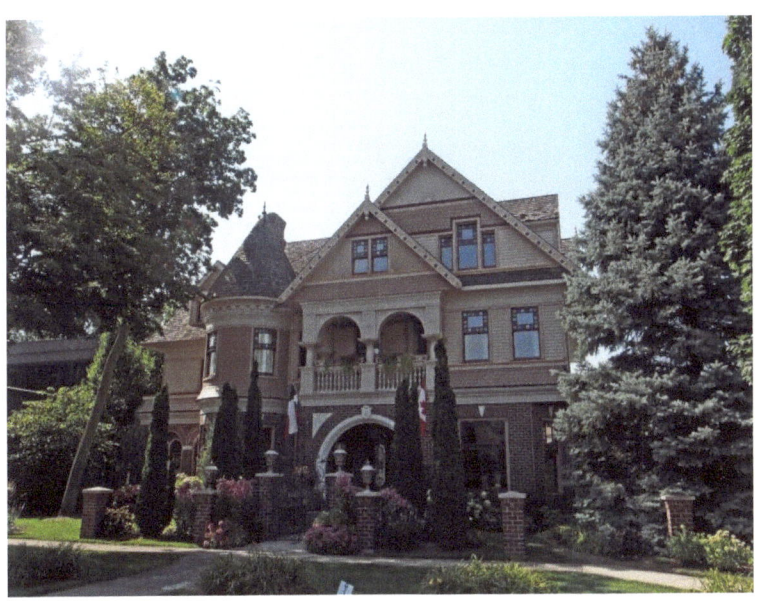

22 Bayview Drive – arched entranceway with a pillared open balustrade balcony above; verge board trim and finials on gables; two storey turret, dormers

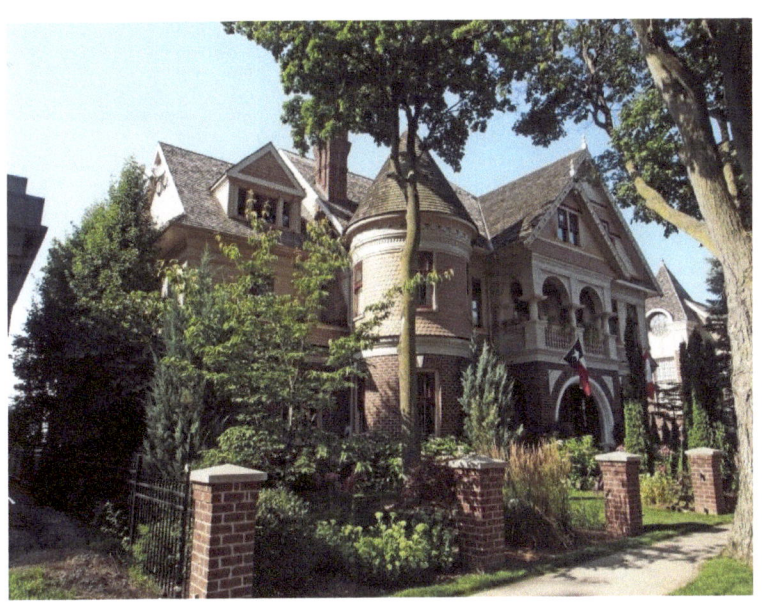

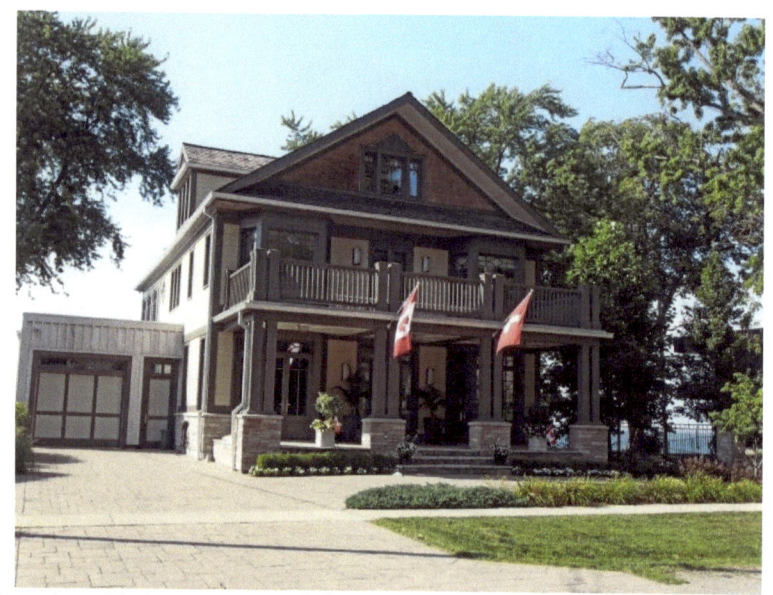

Bayview Drive – second floor full-width balcony, Palladian window in gable, bay windows, dormer

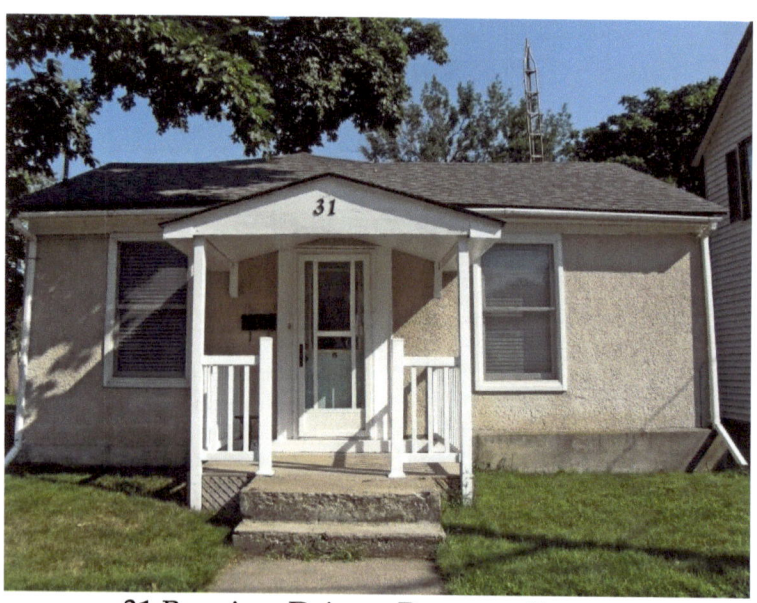

31 Bayview Drive – Regency Cottage

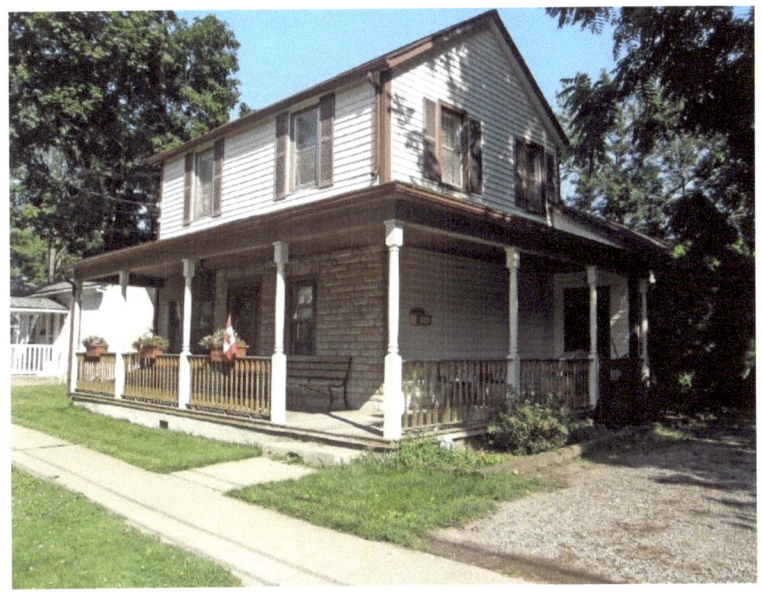

33 Bayview Drive

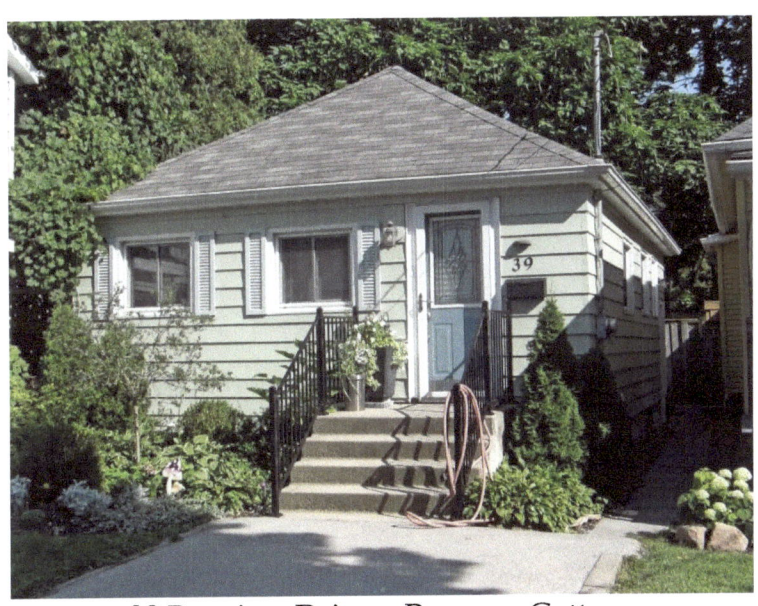

39 Bayview Drive – Regency Cottage

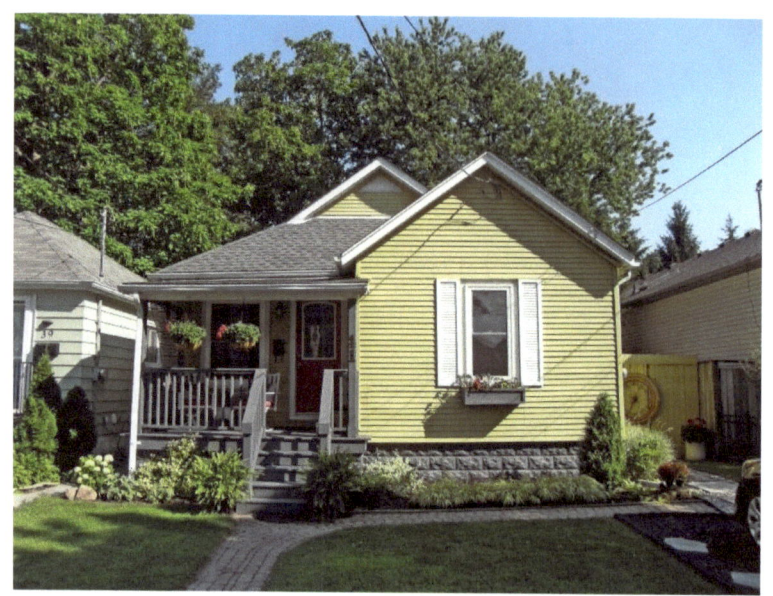
41 Bayview Drive

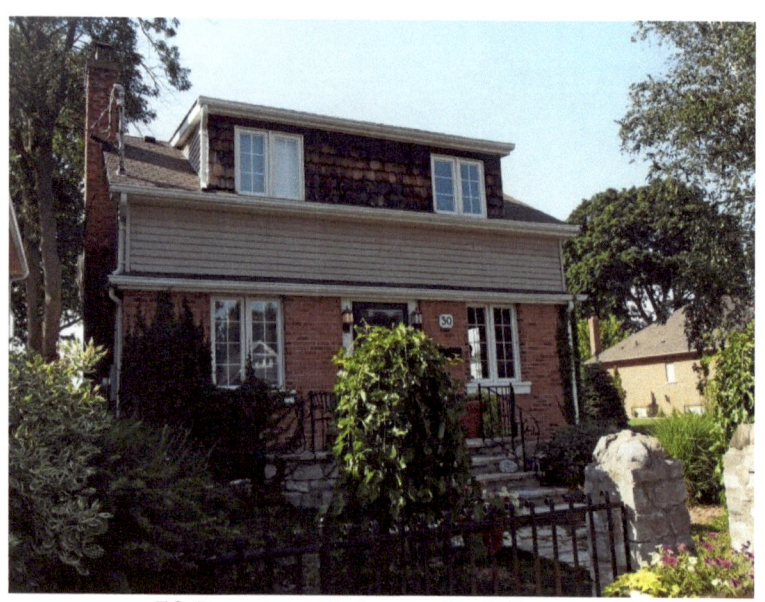
50 Bayview Drive – shed dormer

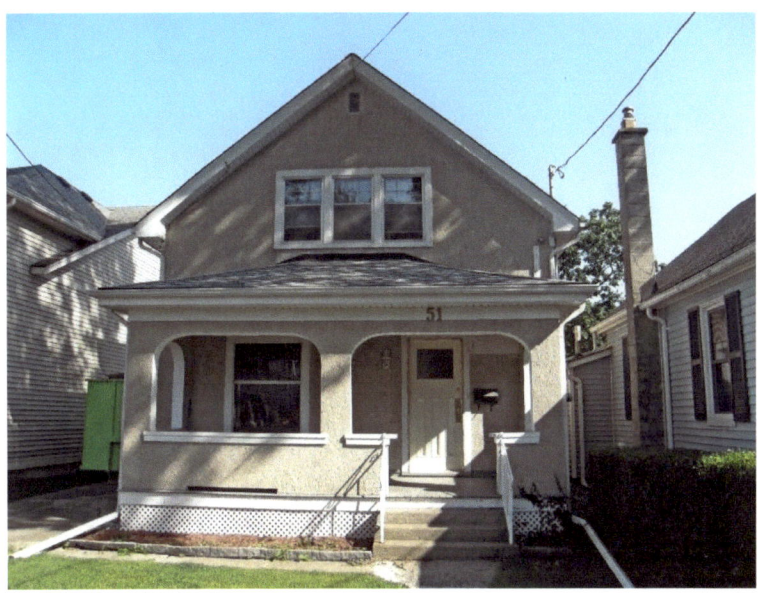

51 Bayview Drive

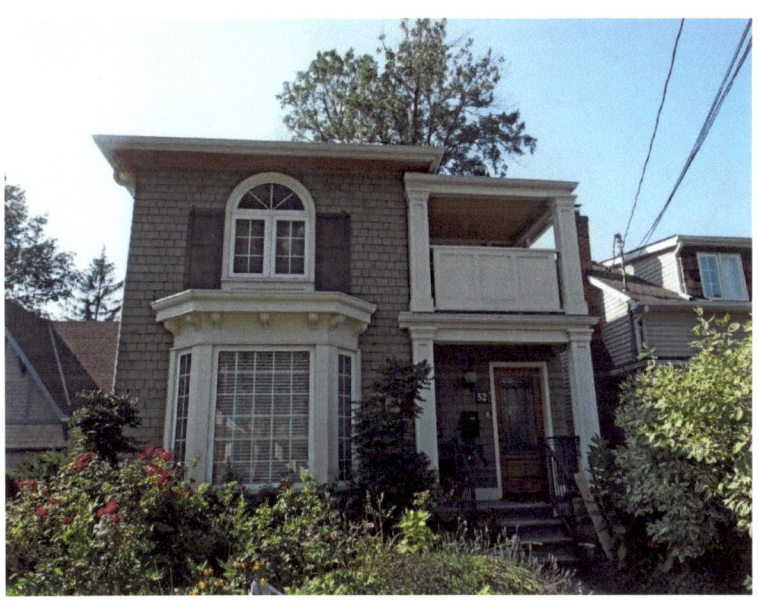

52 Bayview Drive – bay window

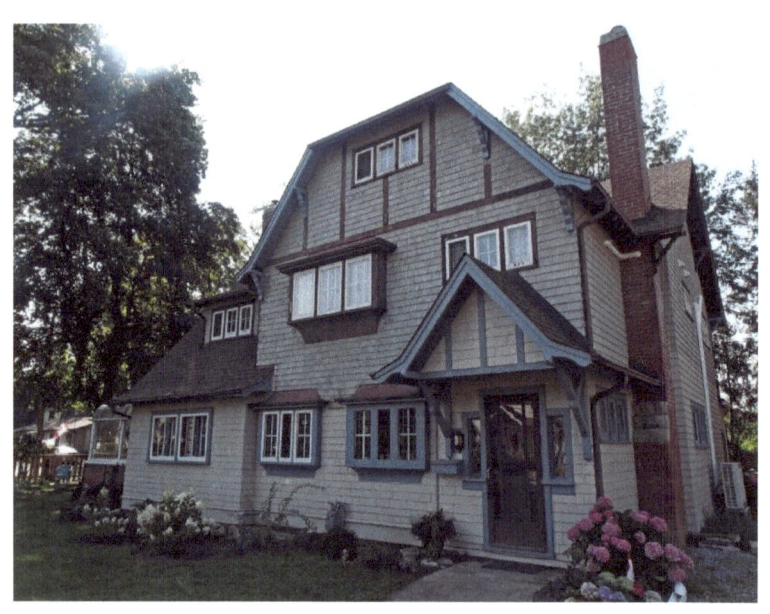

56 Bayview Drive – chipped gable, Tudor half-timbering

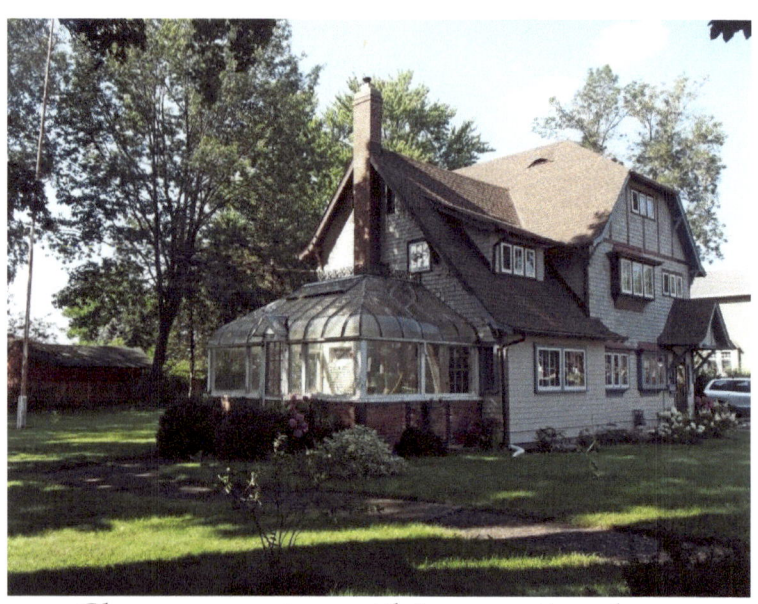

Glass conservatory with iron cresting above

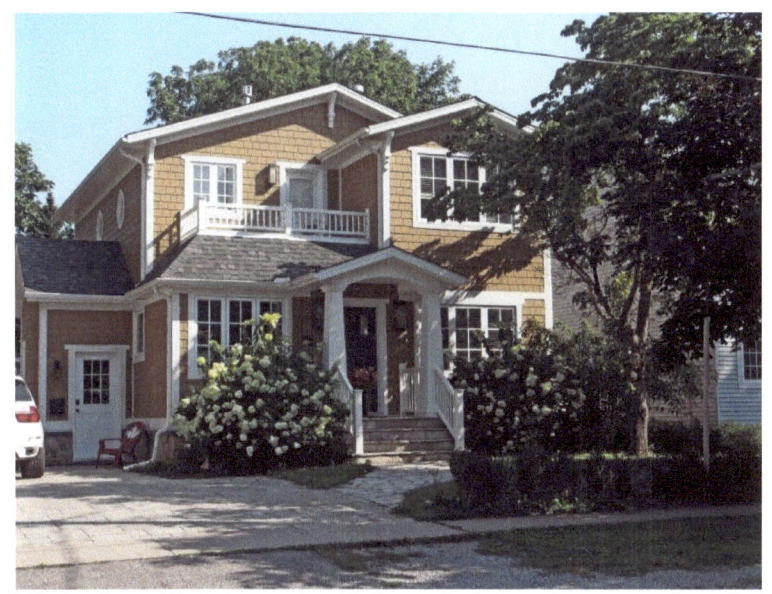

71 Bayview Drive – second floor balcony, cornice brackets

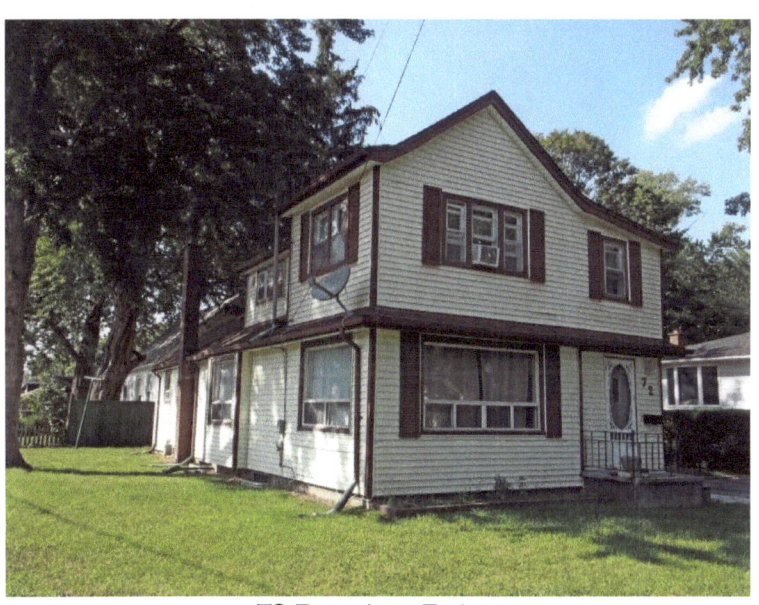

72 Bayview Drive

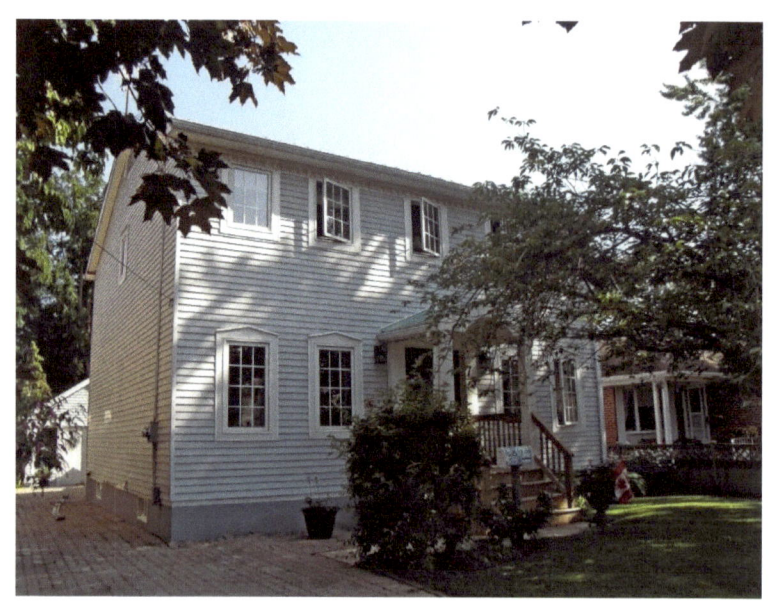

73 Bayview Drive

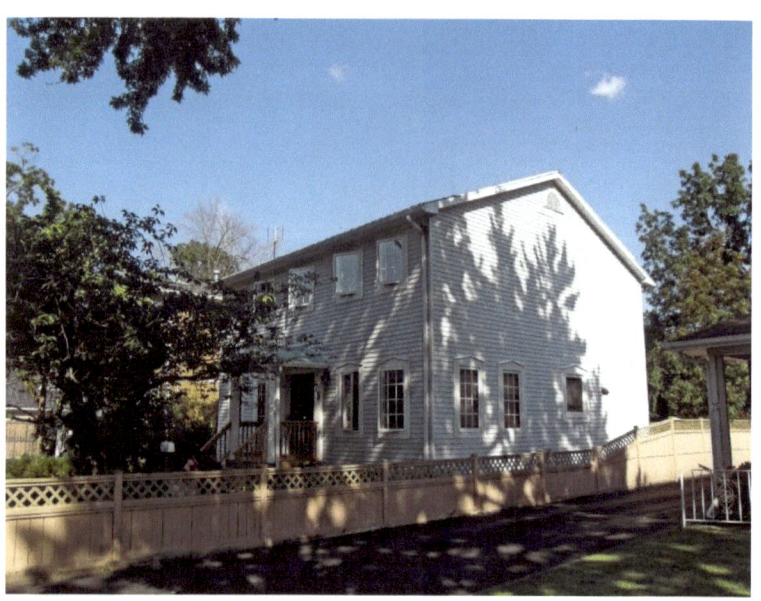

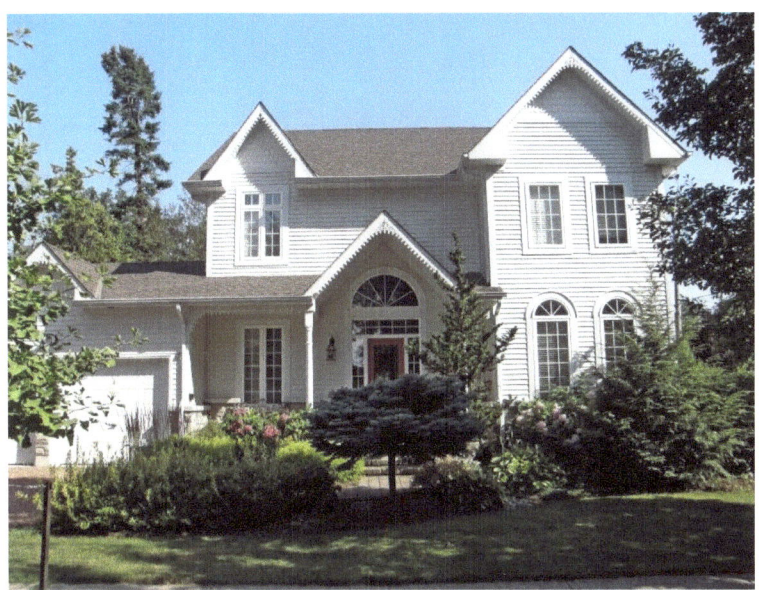
Bayview Drive

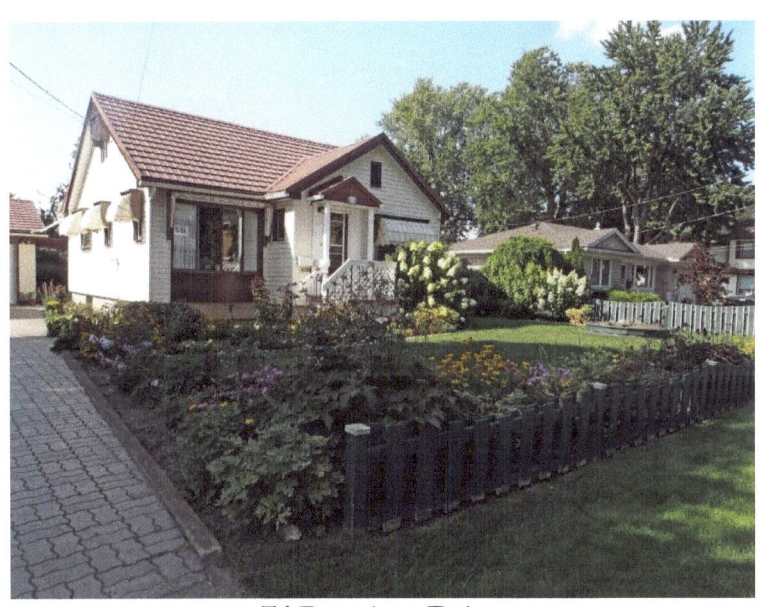
76 Bayview Drive

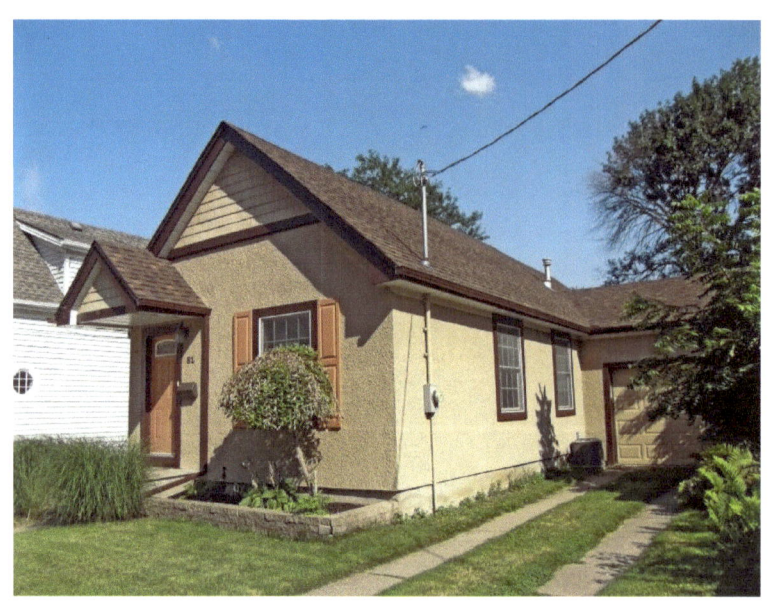

81 Bayview Drive

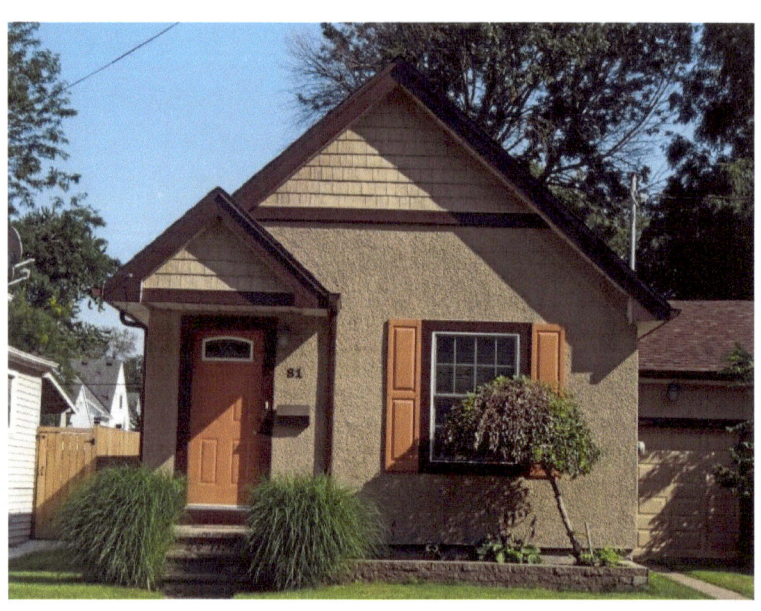

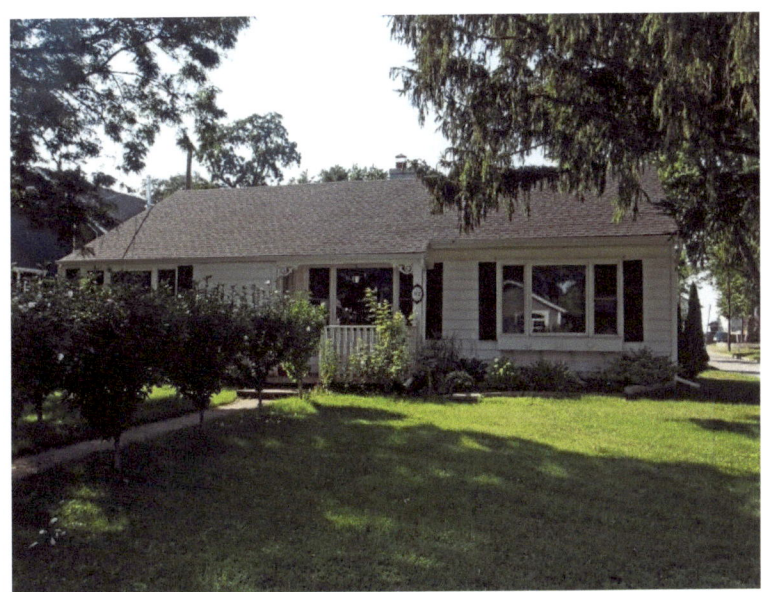

82 Bayview Drive – Regency Cottage

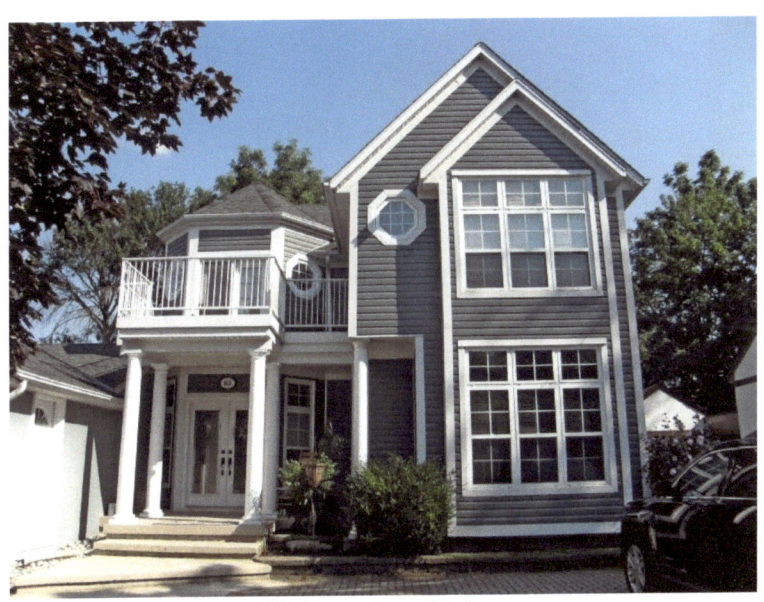

83 Bayview Drive

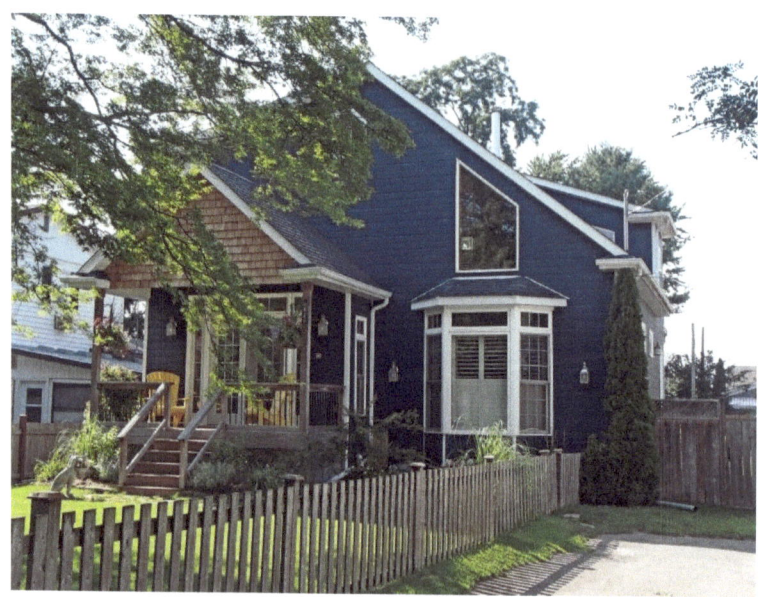
86 Bayview Drive – bay window, shed dormer

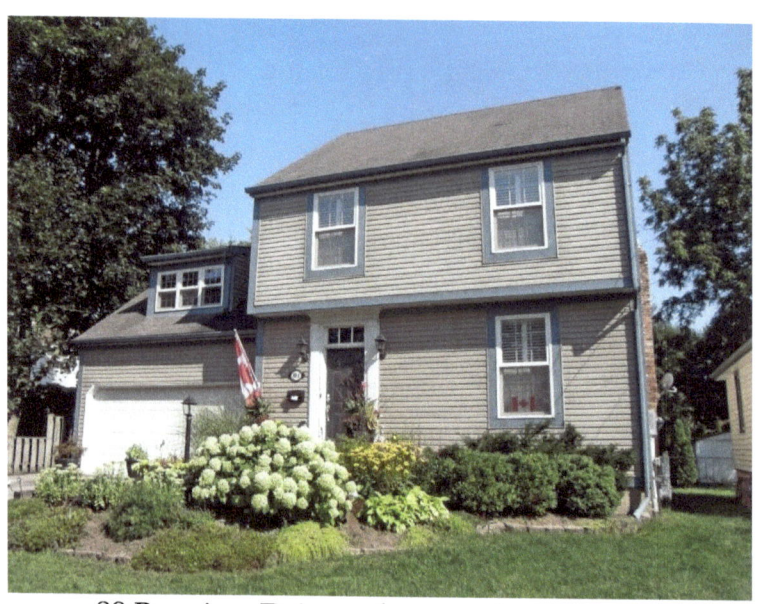
89 Bayview Drive – dormer above garage

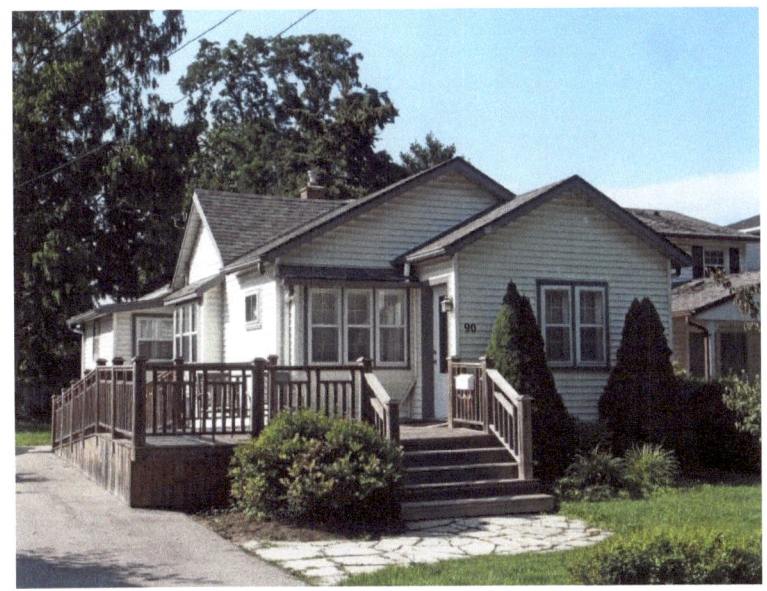

90 Bayview Drive

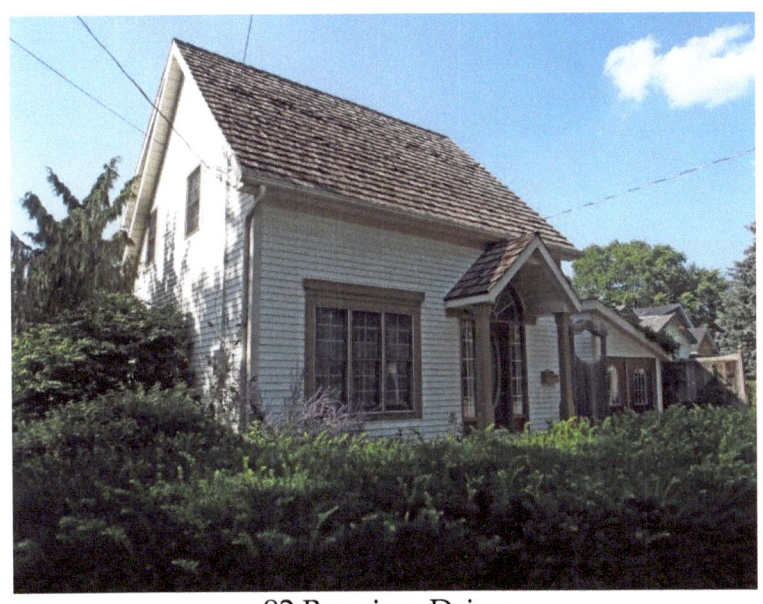

92 Bayview Drive

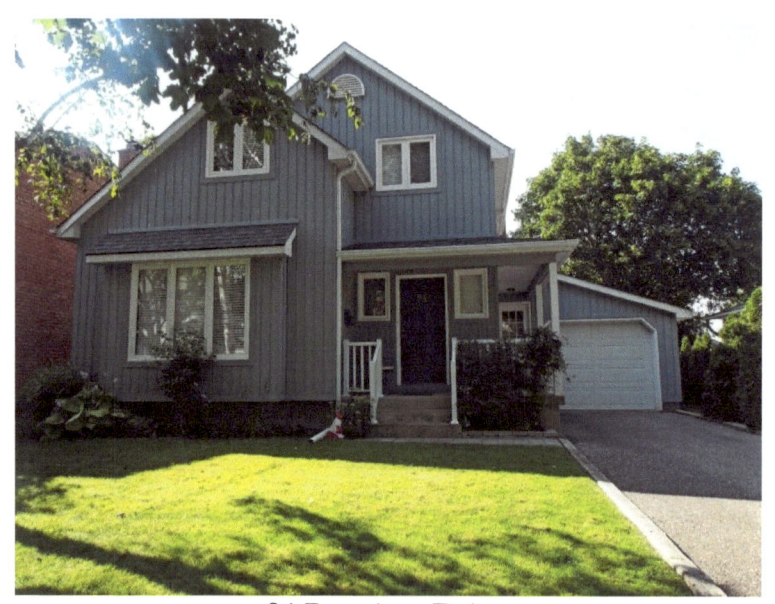
94 Bayview Drive

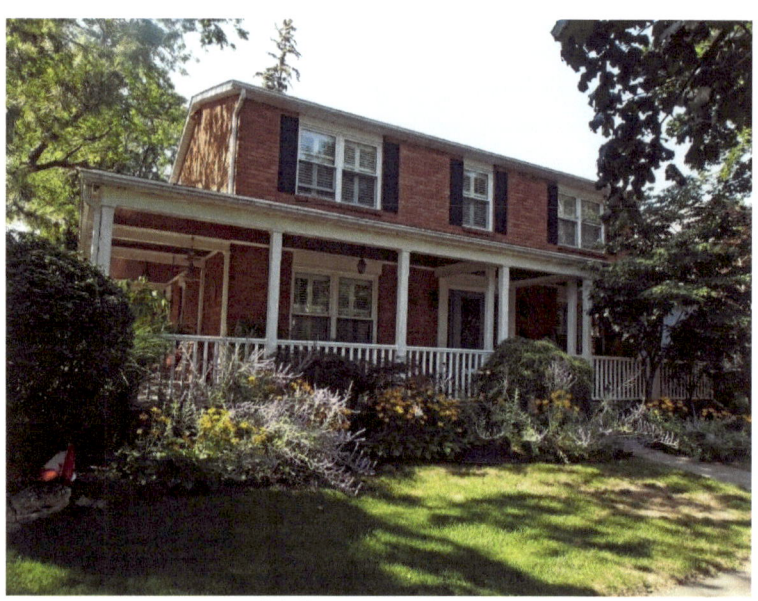
96 Bayview Drive

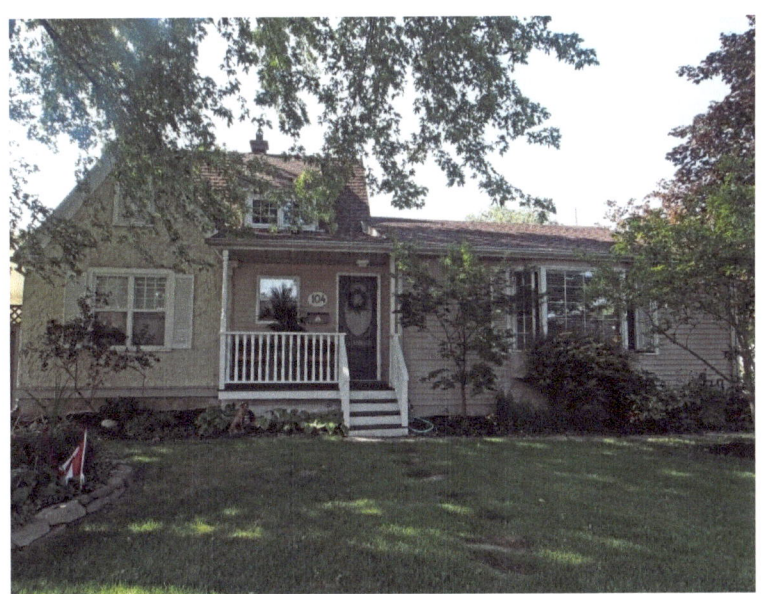

104 Bayview Drive

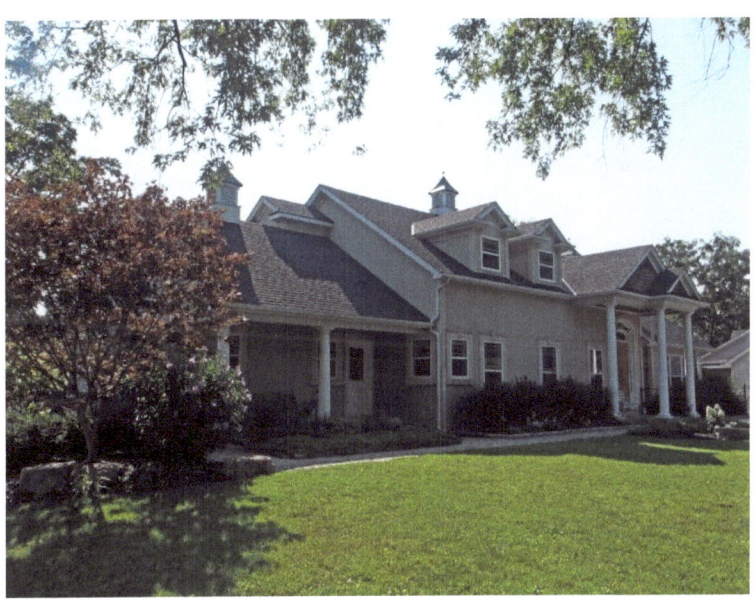

Bayview Drive – dormers, Doric pillars

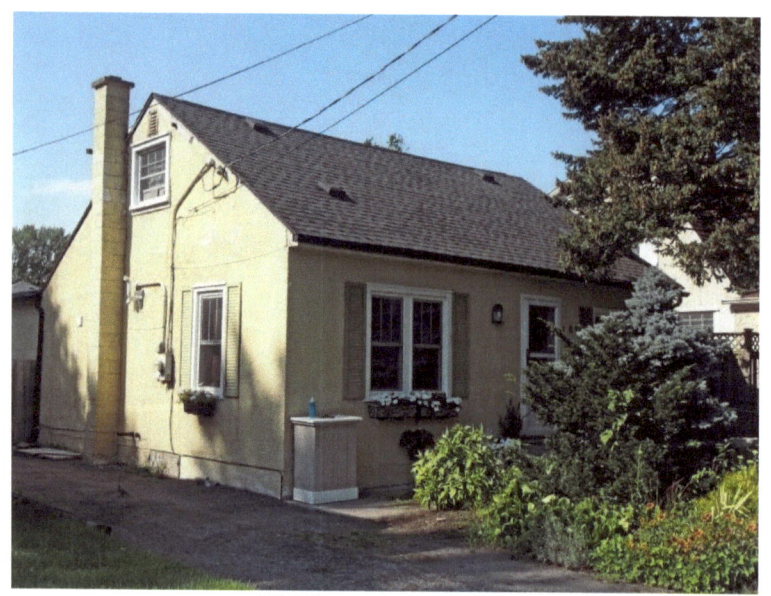
106 Bayview Drive

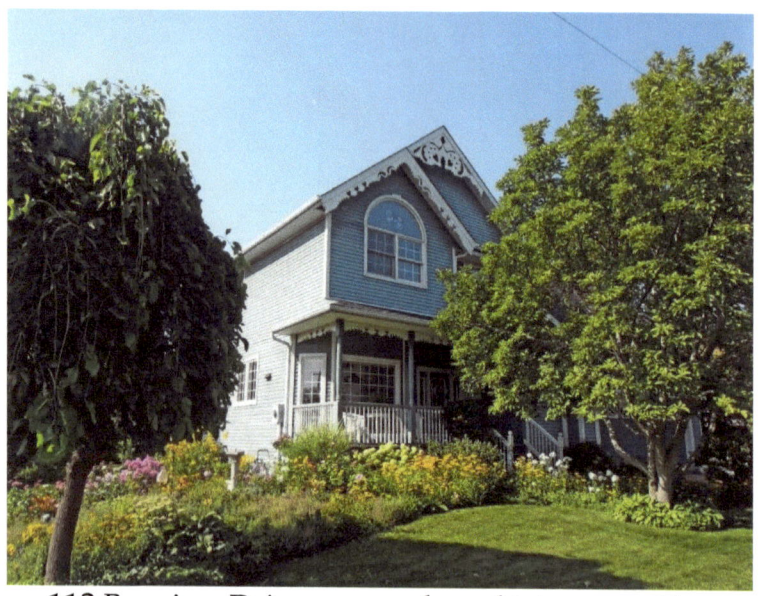
112 Bayview Drive – verge board trim on gables

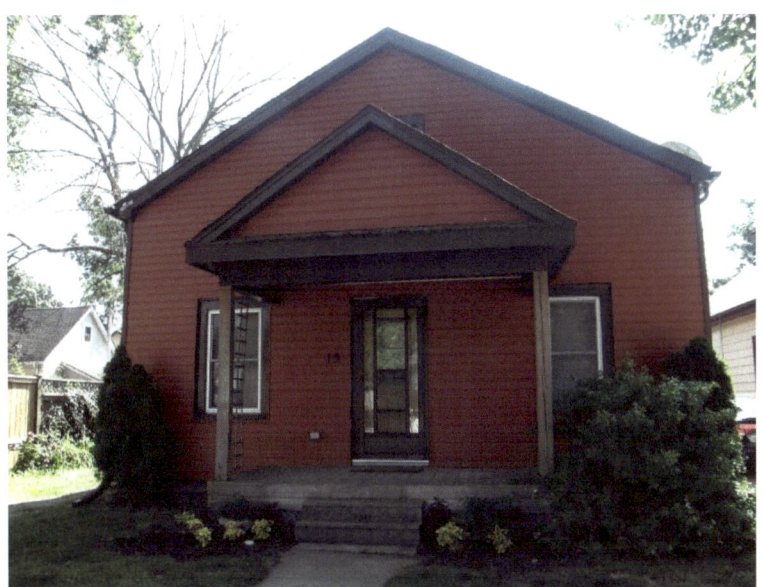

15 Christie Street

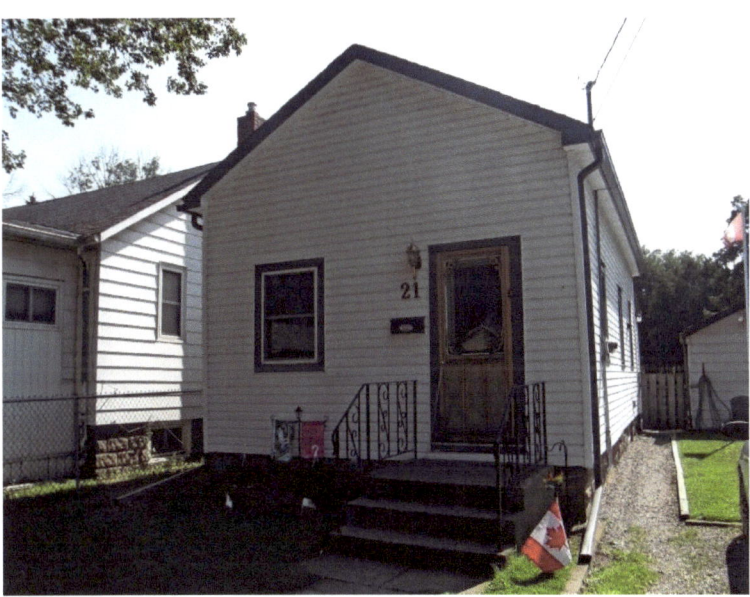

21 Christie Street

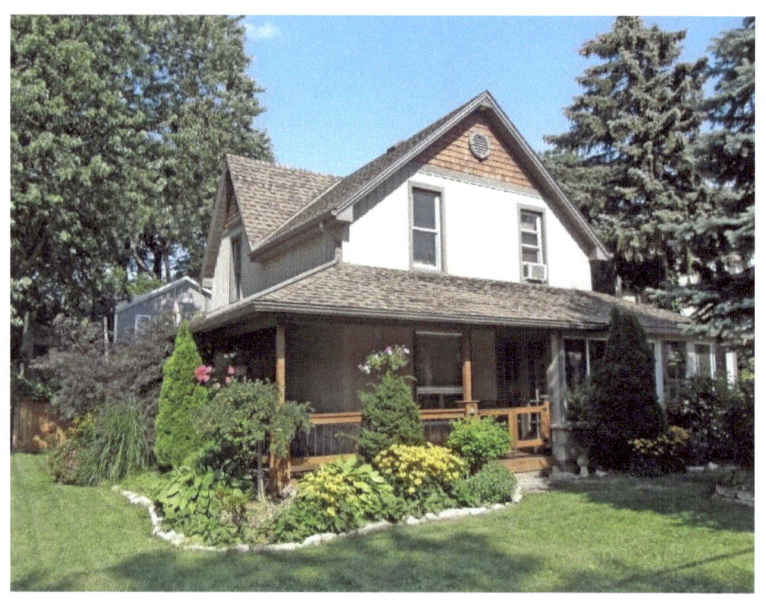

26 Christie Street

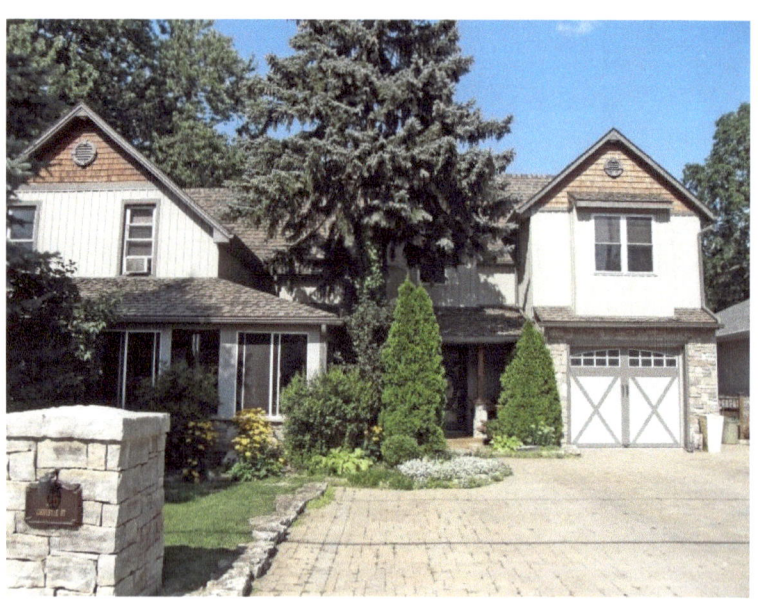

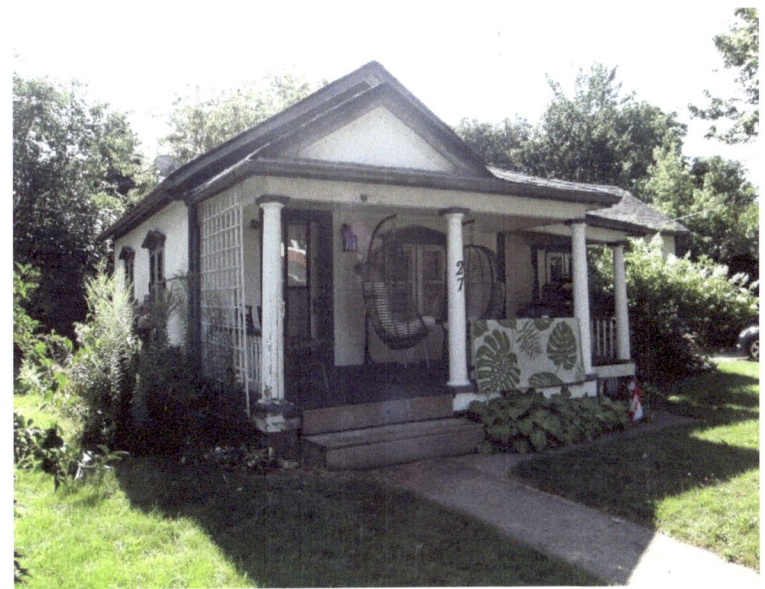

27 Christie Street – Regency Cottage

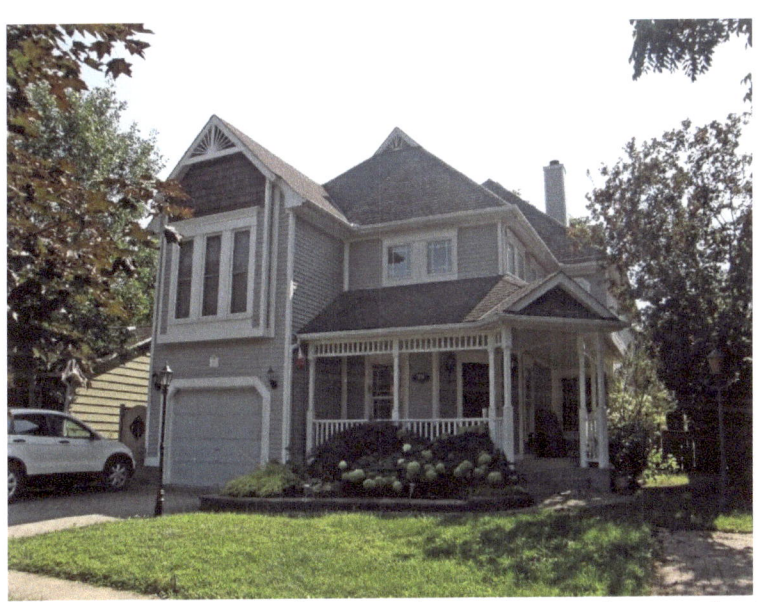

39 Christie Street – matching sunburst pattern in top of gable and tip of roof, pediment

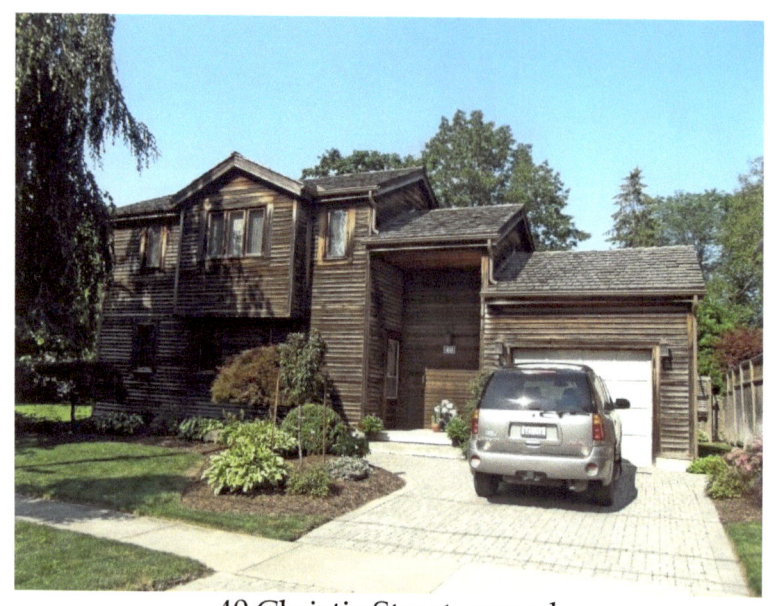
40 Christie Street - wood

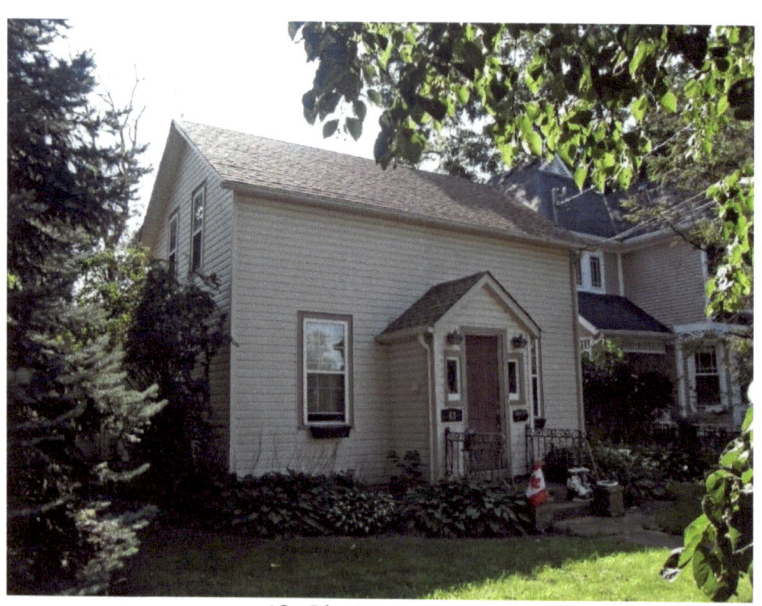
43 Christie Street

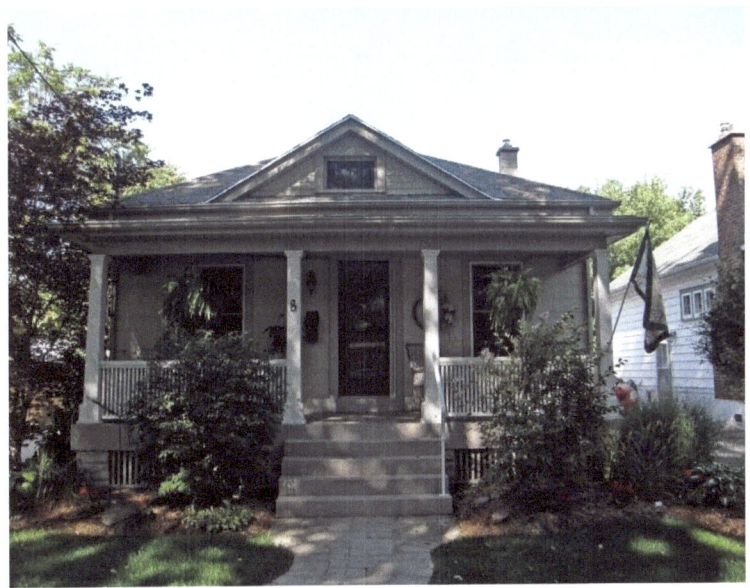

8 Johnston Street – Regency Cottage

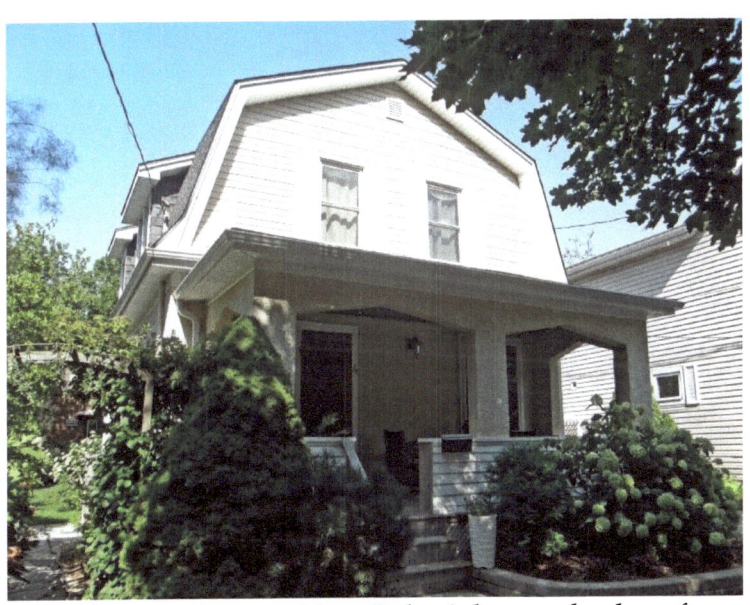

Johnston Street – Neo-Colonial – gambrel roof

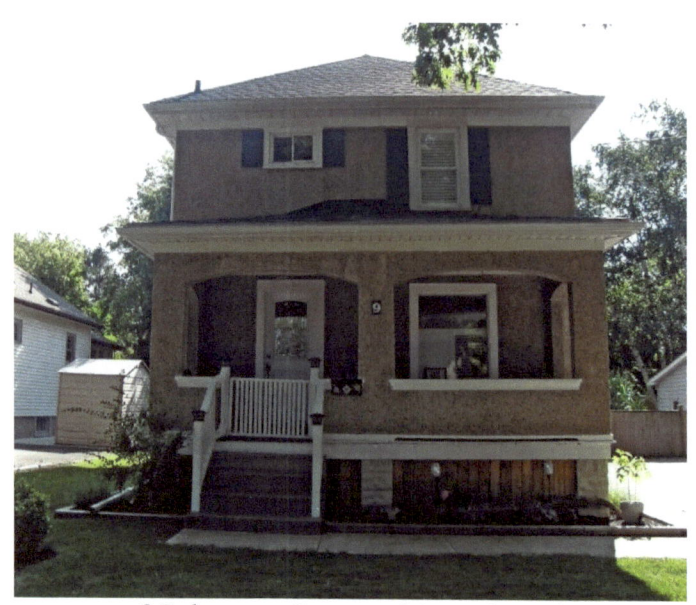

9 Johnston Street – hipped roof

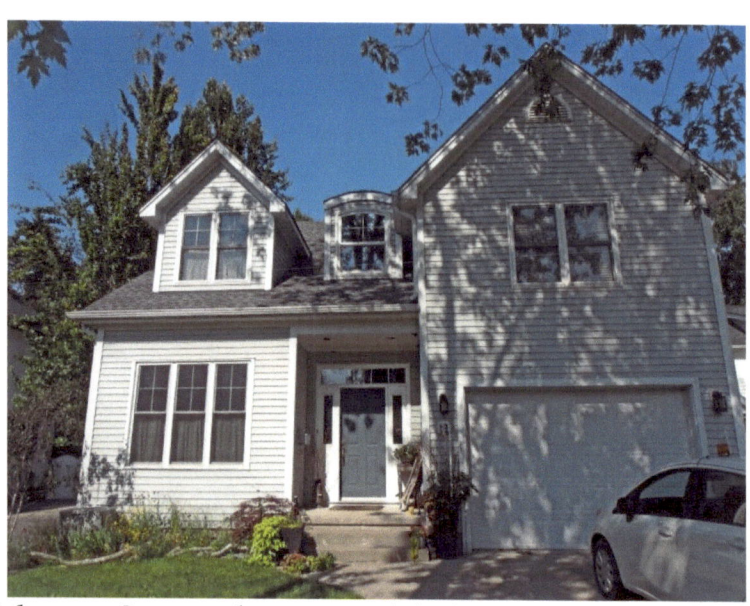

18 Johnston Street – dormers, sidelights and transom windows around door

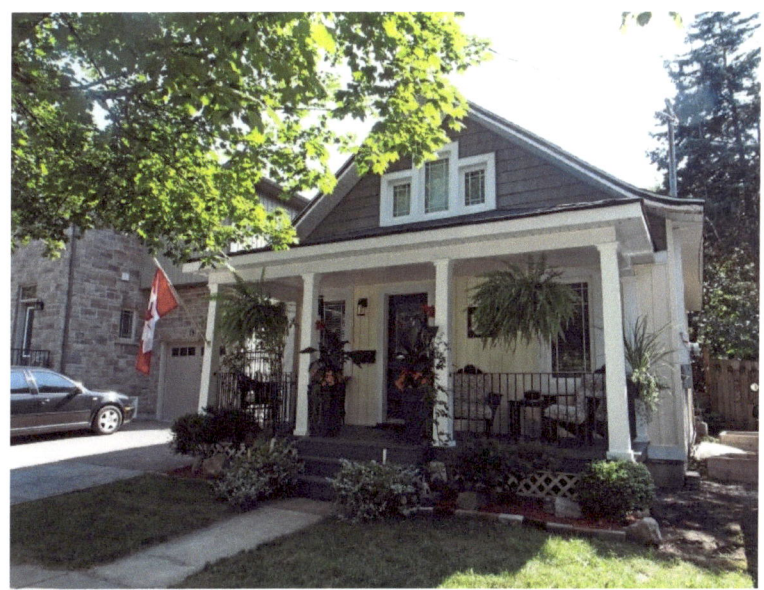

19 Johnston Street – Palladian window in gable

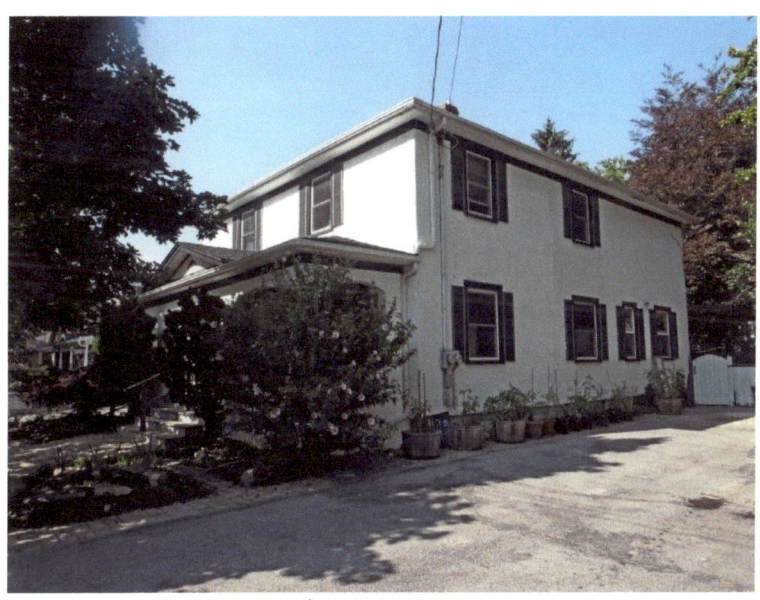

Johnston Street

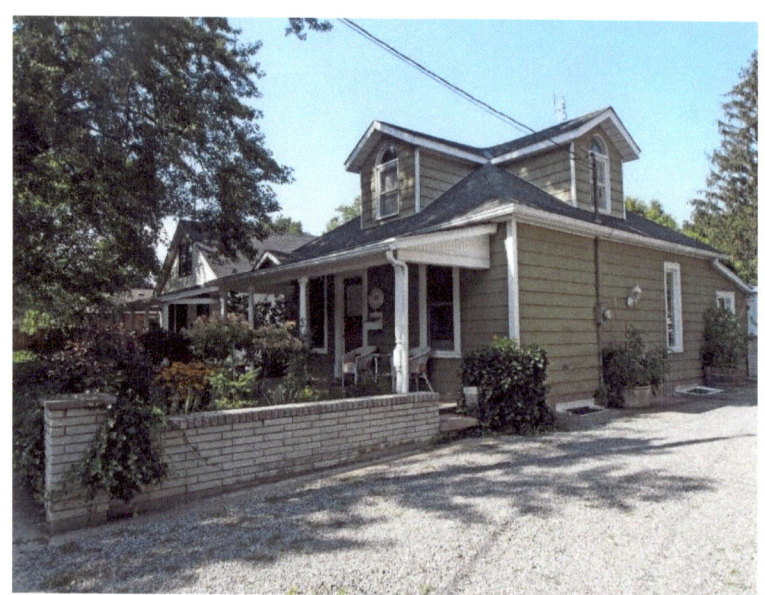

24 Johnston Street - dormers

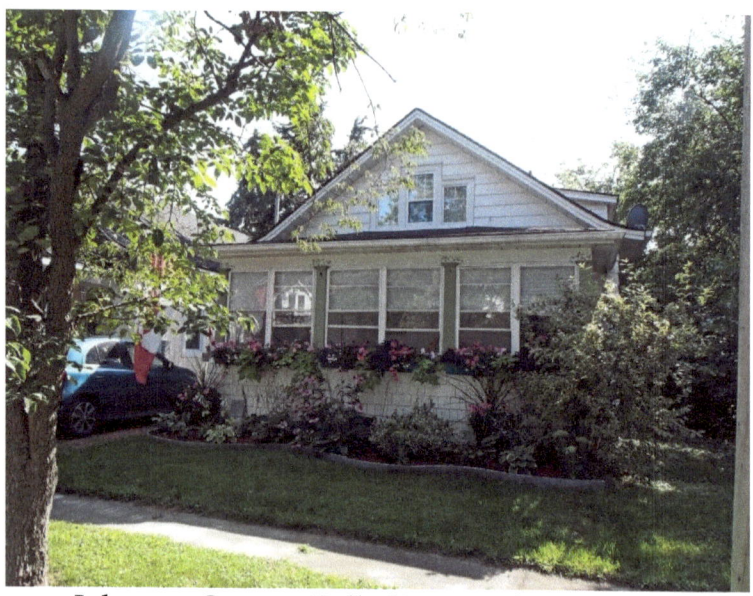

Johnston Street – Palladian window in gable

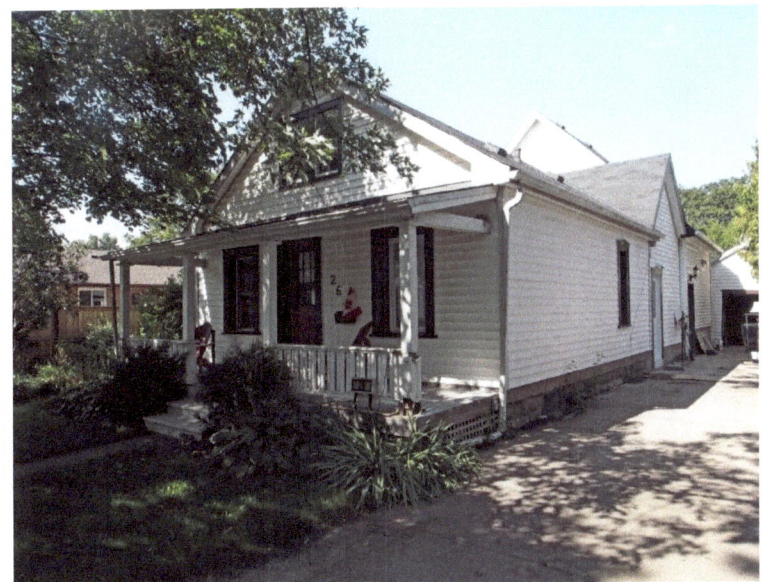

26 Johnston Street

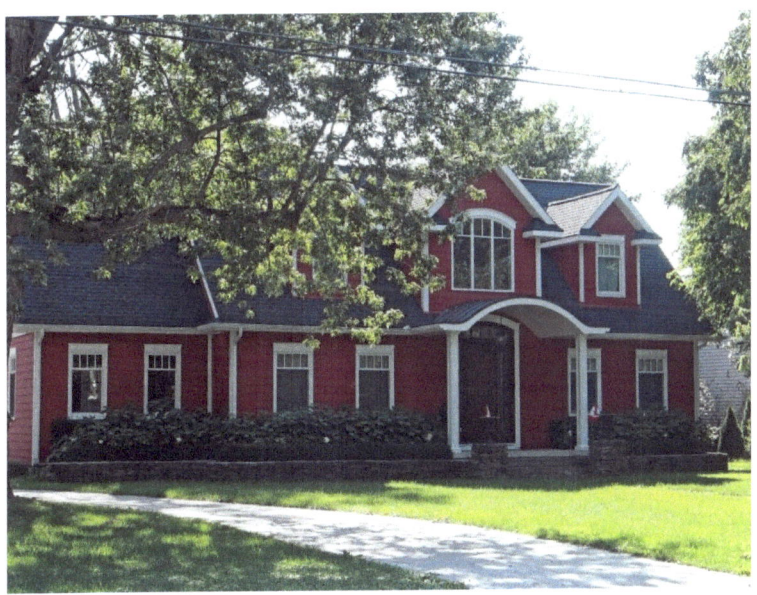

Johnston Street

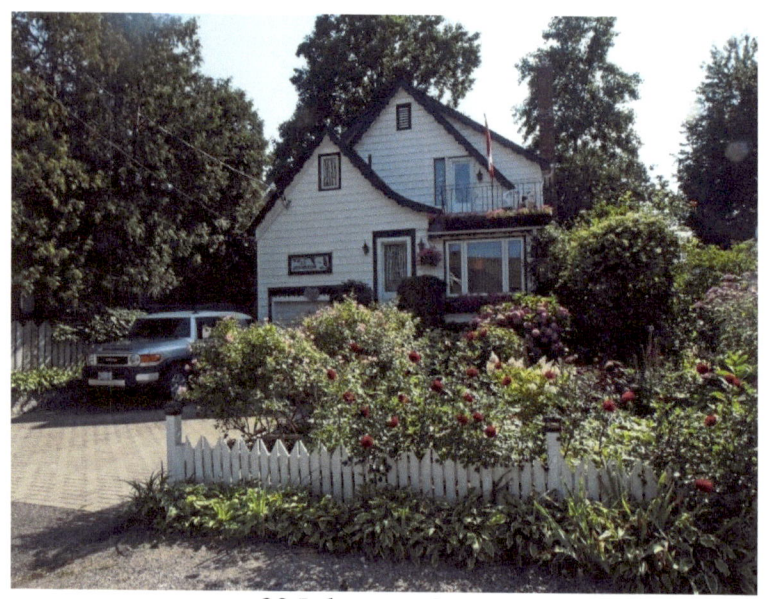

33 Johnston Street

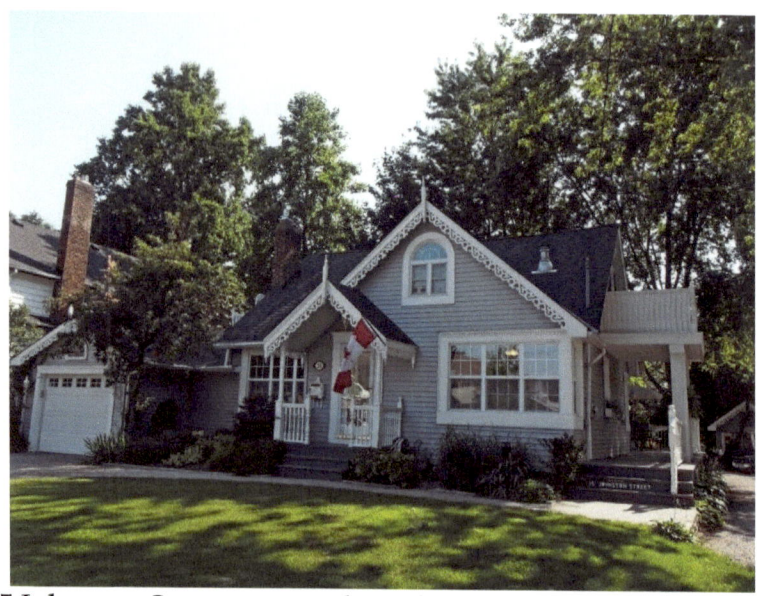

35 Johnston Street – verge board trim and finials on gables

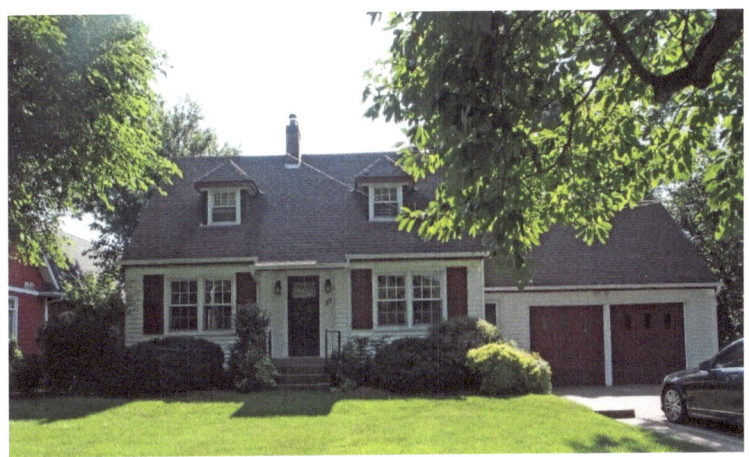

39 Johnston Street

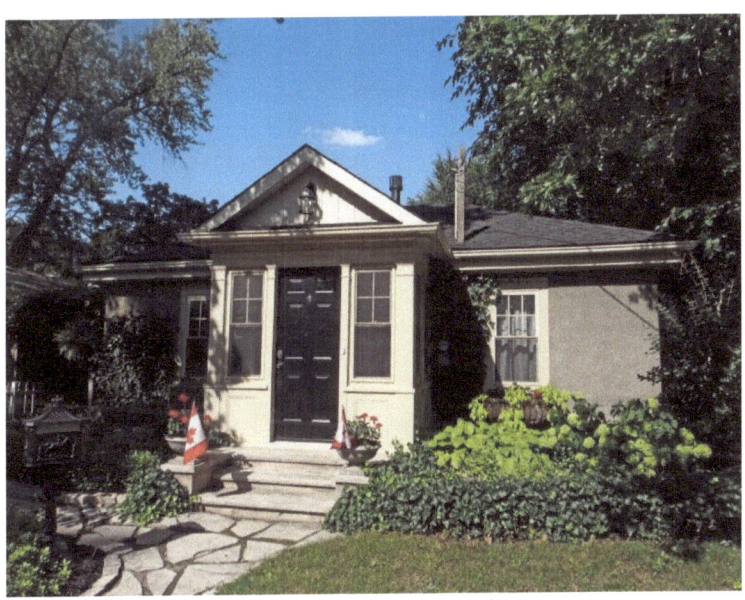

46 Johnston Street - pediment

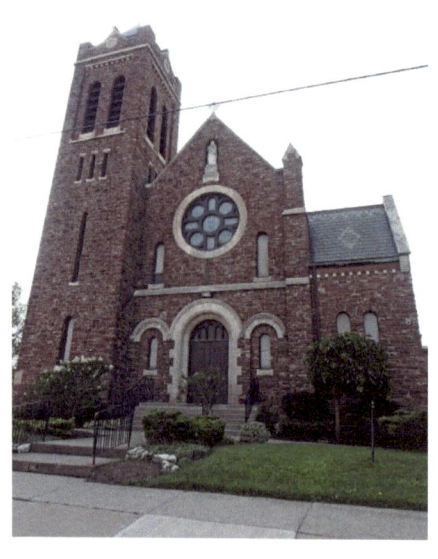

169 St. Paul Crescent - St. Mary of Assumption Roman Catholic Church – 1867 – Romanesque style in sandstone, rose window, buttresses, patterned tile work on the roof

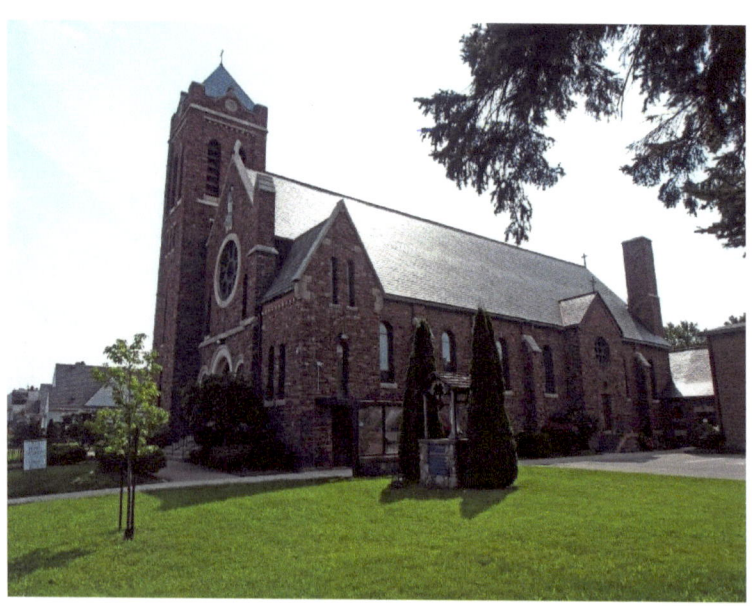

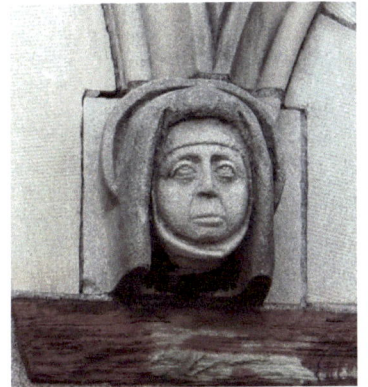 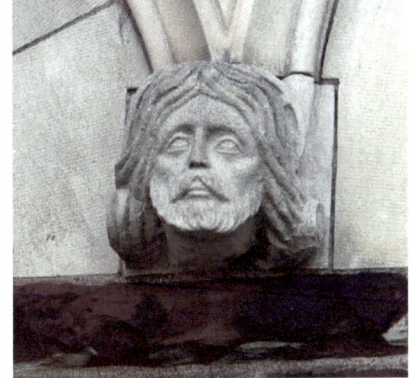

Agraffe at bottom of drip molds

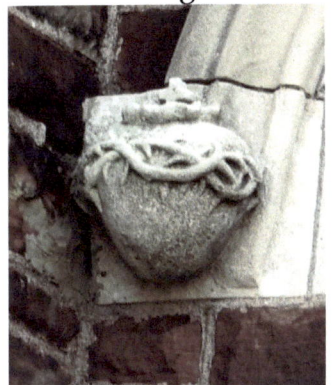 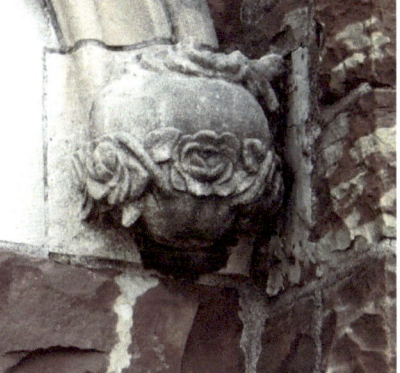

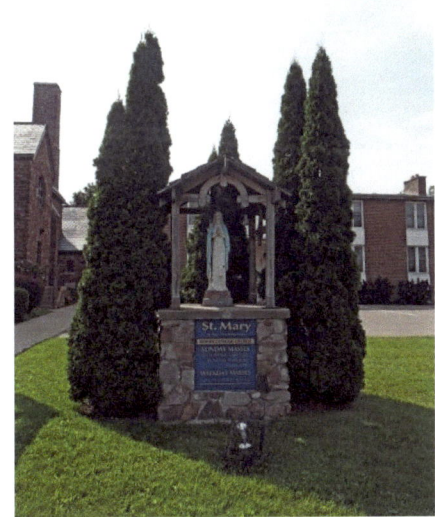

Grotto

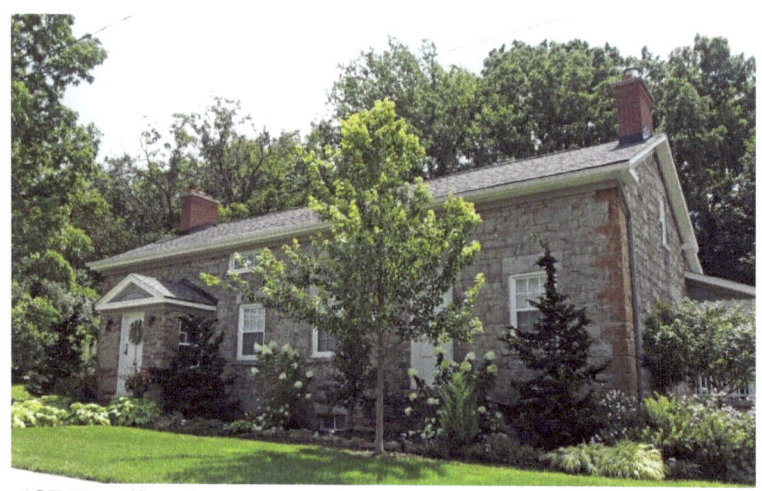

135 Bradley Street was built about 1849-1851 and was originally used as a semi-detached Lock tender's House and was located adjacent to the second Welland Canal. It is a one-and-a-half storey dwelling built of local sandstone laid in random coursing with dressed limestone quoins at the corners. In the backyard of the property there used to be a quarry and some of the stone that was used on the Second Welland Canal was quarried here.

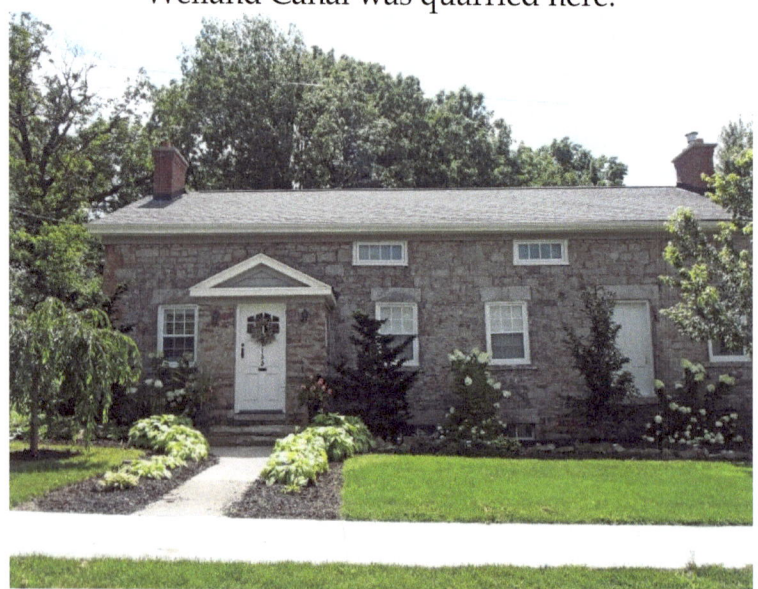

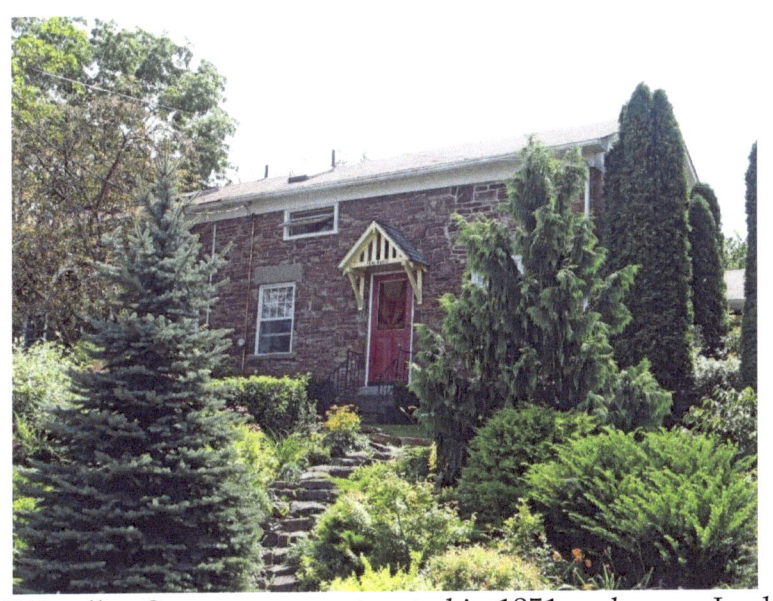

77 Bradley Street was constructed in 1851 and was a Lock tender's House providing accommodations for men tending the locks of the Welland Canal. The semi-detached, one-and-a-half storey dwelling was built of sandstone cut from a quarry close to the house. It is accented with limestone corner quoins and stone lintels and sills. Lock tenders aided the navigation of ships through the Welland Canals.

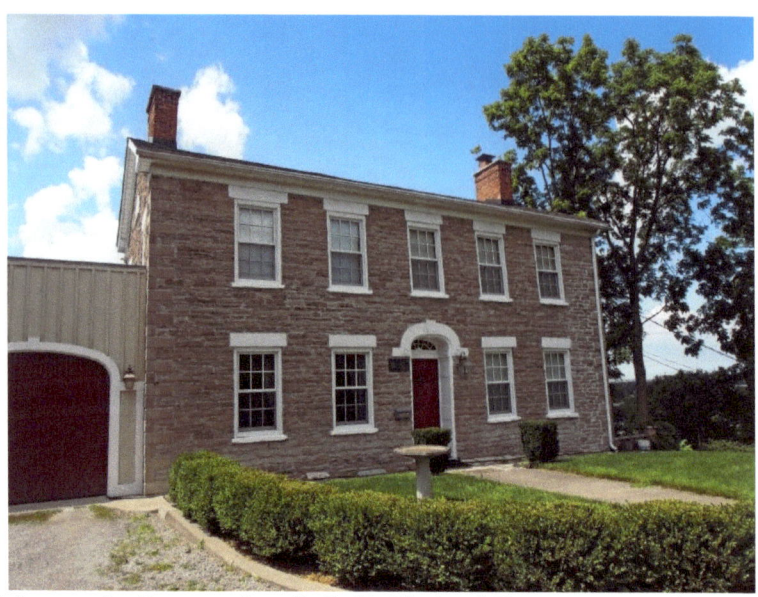

51 Mountain Street - Jacob Ball, United Empire Loyalist – circa 1824. The original stone portion of this house has a two-storey, five bay aspect facing the driveway. The main façade is of split face ashlar coursing with cut stone quoins. The sidewalls are of a more random coursing and all stone is local. All the windows have solid stone sills, some with solid stone lintels and others with a flat arch of the same local stone. The land on which the building is located was originally a Crown Grant to George Ball in 1796. The property was sold to the Public Works Department in 1843 and was then turned over to the Welland Canal Loan Company. During this period, the building was used as the home of the lockmaster, overseeing the work of seventeen lock tenders.

Although the first settlers arrived as early as 1783 or 1784, it took decades for the area to grow and develop into one of the most significant areas in the Niagara region. In 1858, the four communities in Grantham Township of Centreville, Protestant Hill, Westport and Slabtown became known as Merritton. In 1851 the Welland Canal Loan Company purchased the location and transformed it into an industrial hub capable of housing mills and generating valuable water power. The opportunities to develop these industries created immense growth in the Merritton area. During the mid-1800s, the issues of transportation and accessibility were very important for small towns and cities. Merritton had a number of advantages that made it more accessible than many other towns. The Great Western Railway provided excellent passenger service to the area with a station located in Merritton and running regular routes from Niagara Falls. The first inter-urban electric streetcar in North America was operated in Merritton in 1887 linking Merritton with St. Catharines. The canal ran through the town and Merritton grew quickly.

On January 1, 1861 Merritton was amalgamated with the City of St. Catharines. The Town Hall became the St. Catharines Historical Museum and is now home to the Merritton Seniors' Centre.

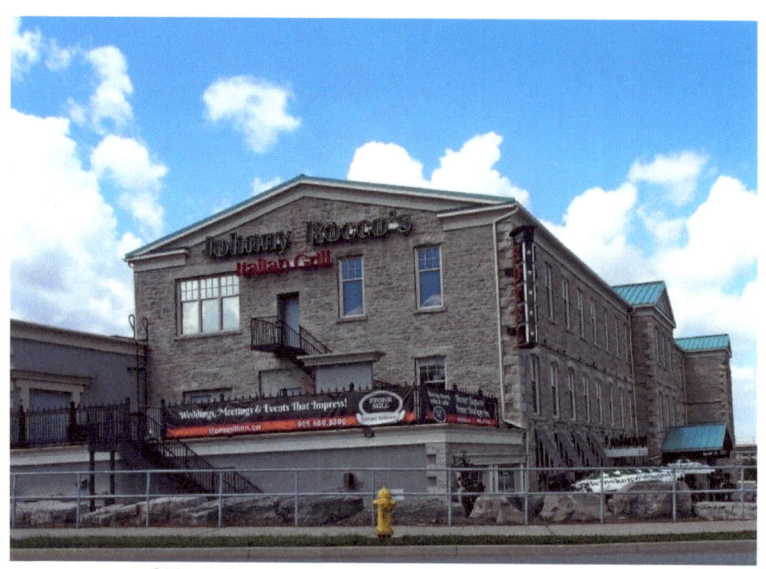

271 Merritt Street – Stone Mill Inn

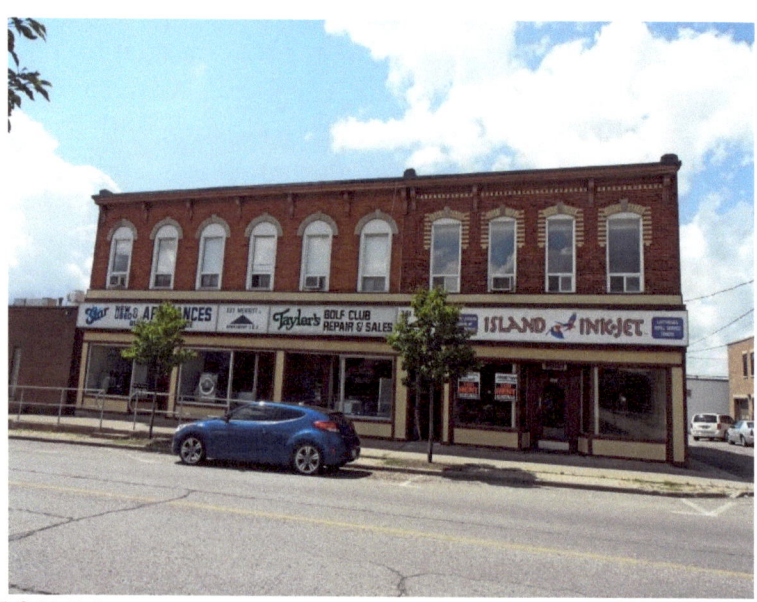

337-341 Merritt Street – keystones and voussoirs, dichromatic brickwork, cornice brackets

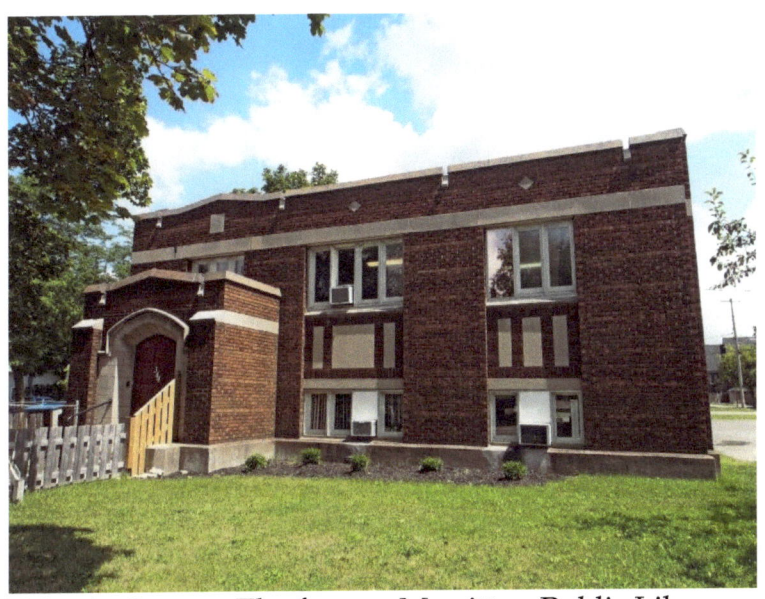

344 Merritt Street – The former Merritton Public Library was built in 1924 through a grant for the Andrew Carnegie Foundation. The building was designed in the Neo-Tudor style by renowned local architect Arthur Nicholson. The front entrance has a large Tudor-arch with decorative buttresses. A decorated parapet surrounds the flat roof and there is a single chimney. The exterior of the building is a dark discolored rough brick. There is a light colored stone frieze around the building located below the diamond shaped stone decorations in the brickwork. The many windows allow a lot of natural light into the building. The windows are surrounded by wooden mullions.

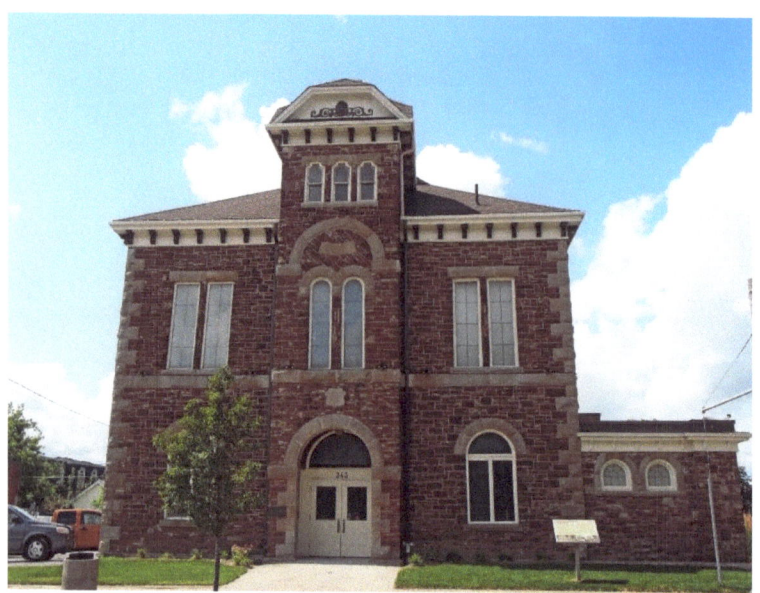

343 Merritt Street – The former Merritton Town Hall was constructed in 1879 by James MacDonald. The building is a rectangular structure made of local sandstone on the exterior. It is described as Victorian architecture with contrasting quoins, a string belt course, and radiating arch voussoirs over the windows and doors. The projecting bell tower has detailed stone work and an interesting shaped roof. The hip roof is trimmed with a boxed cornice with a frieze and brackets. The front double doors have a fan transom and are inset in the centre of the bell tower.

    The building housed municipal offices, a community centre, the mechanics institute, the waterworks commission, and the library. In 1888, the fire department was formed and moved into the building.

    Merritton Town Hall was the hub of the community where town members gathered for dances, concerts and movie showings.

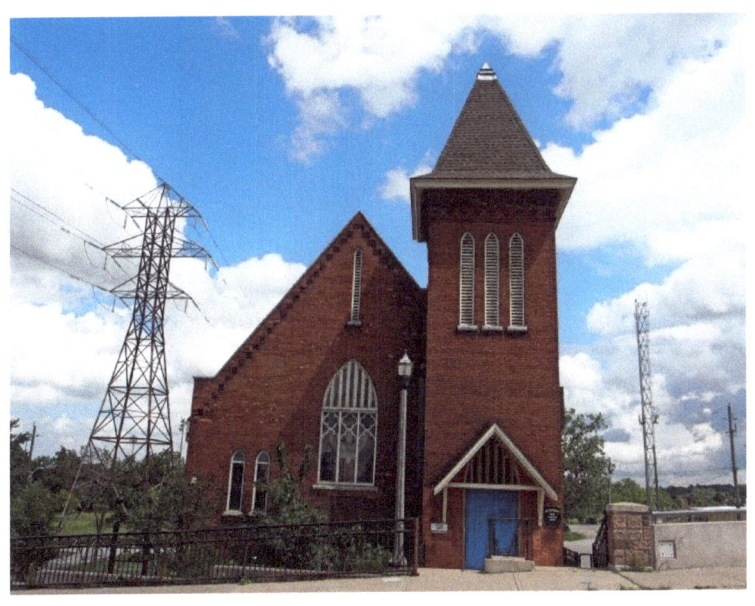

372 Merritt Street – St. Andrew's Church – lancet windows

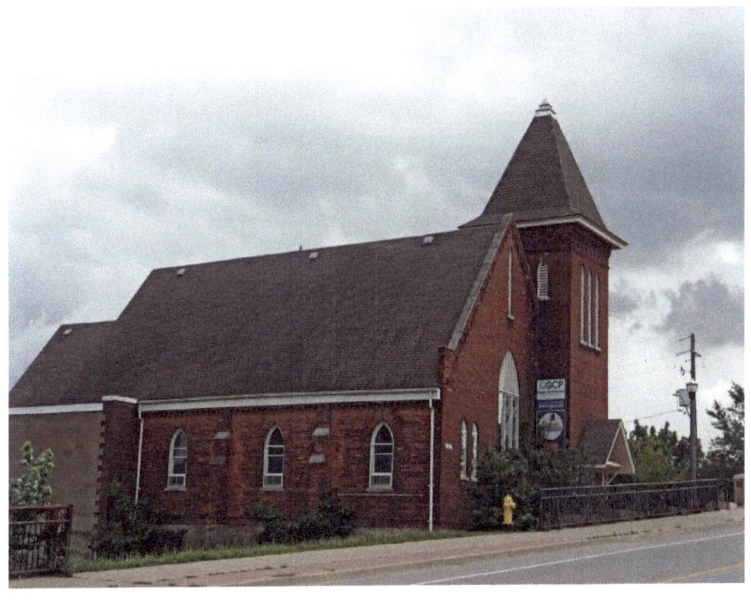

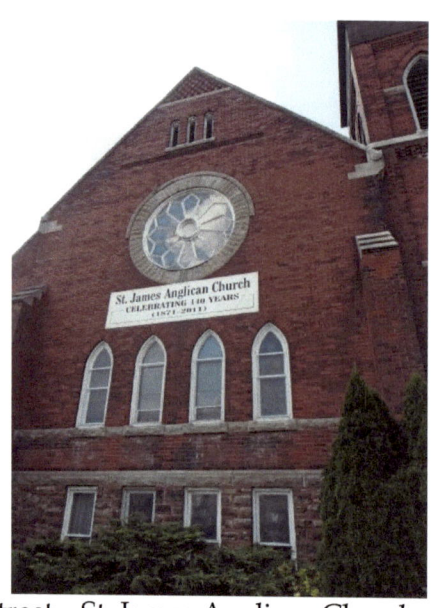

405 Merritt Street – St. James Anglican Church – 1892 – lancet windows, rose window, two-storey tower - After years of history, which included surviving a tornado, it closed on January 22, 2017 because there are not enough people to fill the pews every week and serve itself or the community the way it once did.

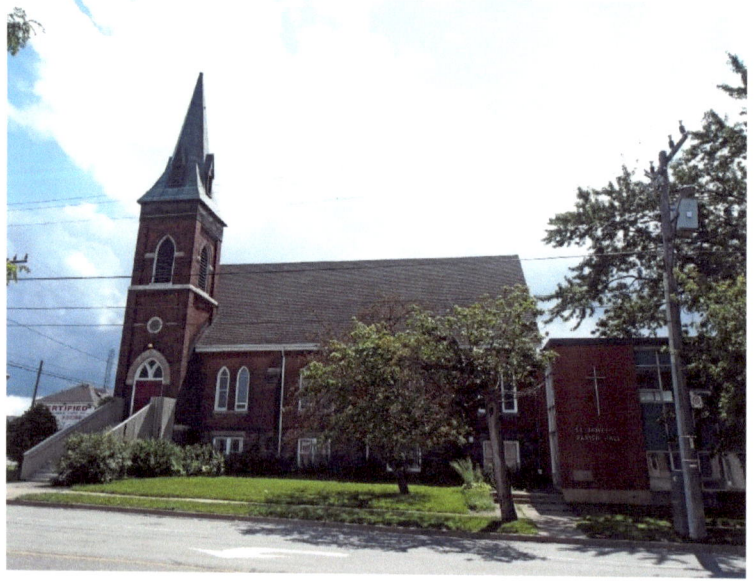

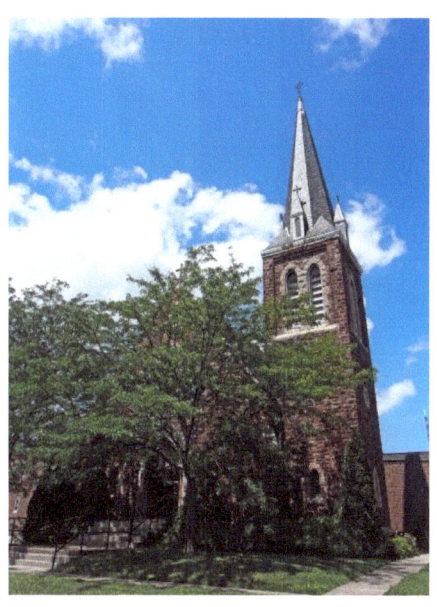

31 Chestnut Street East – St. Patrick's Roman Catholic Church – 1892 – two-storey tower with spire, buttresses, lancet windows

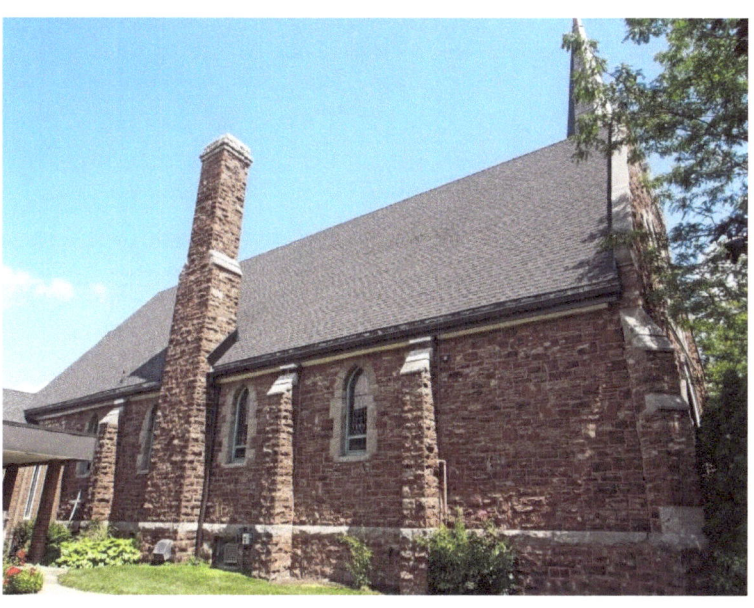

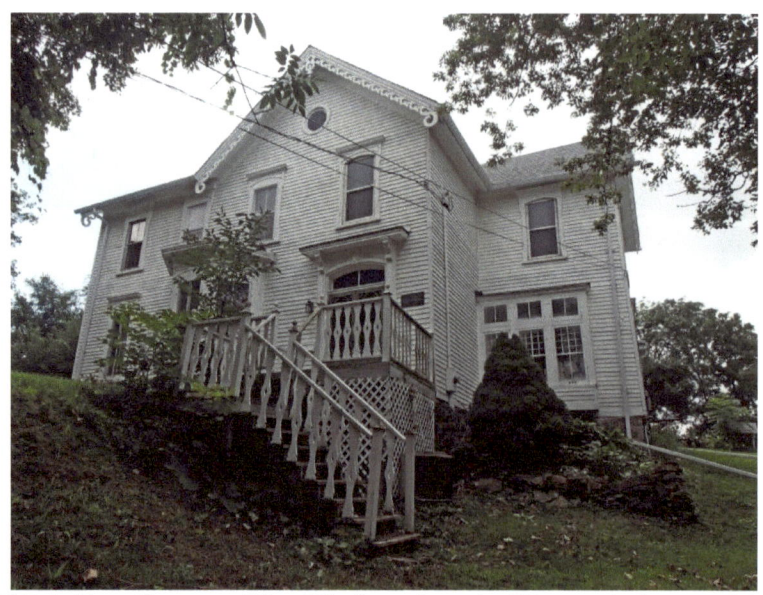

159 Moffatt Street – The Phelps-Austin House is located in a prominent location overlooking the former second Welland Canal and the valley where the original owner, Noah Phelps, operated his sawmill. It is a two-storey frame house with a high cross-gabled roof. Each façade is arranged in a picturesque fashion.

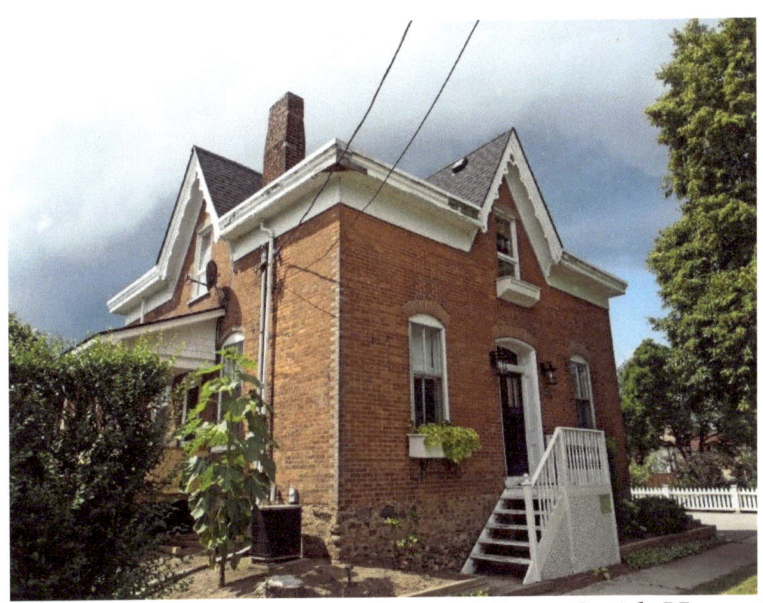

479 Vine Street – The Gibson-McIsaac-Smith House is a 1½ storey brick veneer home built around 1870. It has a hipped roof with boxed cornice and frieze. All of the windows are double hung in a two over two pane arrangement. Above the door is a segmental transom which opens for ventilation.

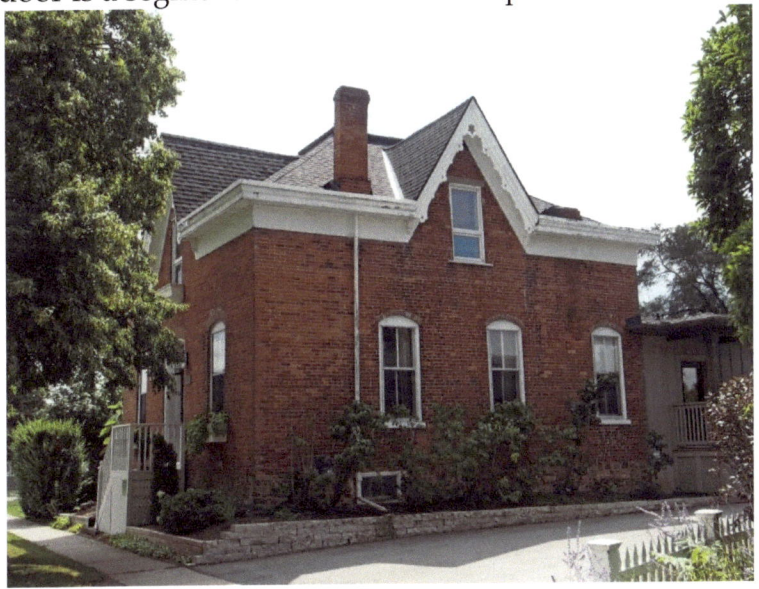

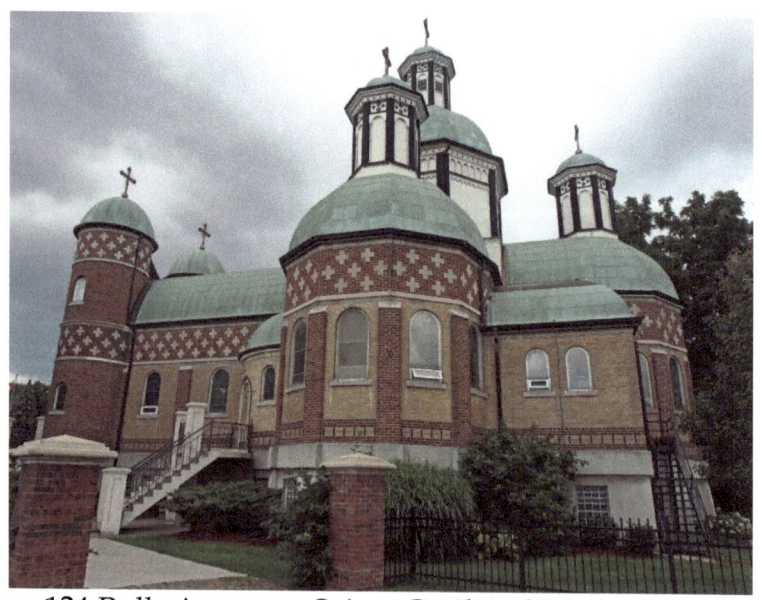

124 Rolls Avenue – Saints Cyril and Methodius Ukrainian Catholic Church – The style is Byzantine Revival which is typified by domes, decorative brickwork and stone arches. The plan of the building is typical church cruciform with a main rectangular body (nave) crossed by a transept. There are six multi-sided domes on the roof. The elaborate detailing is characteristic of this style and features seven different colours and textures of brick and stone executed mainly as varying heights of bands around the building.

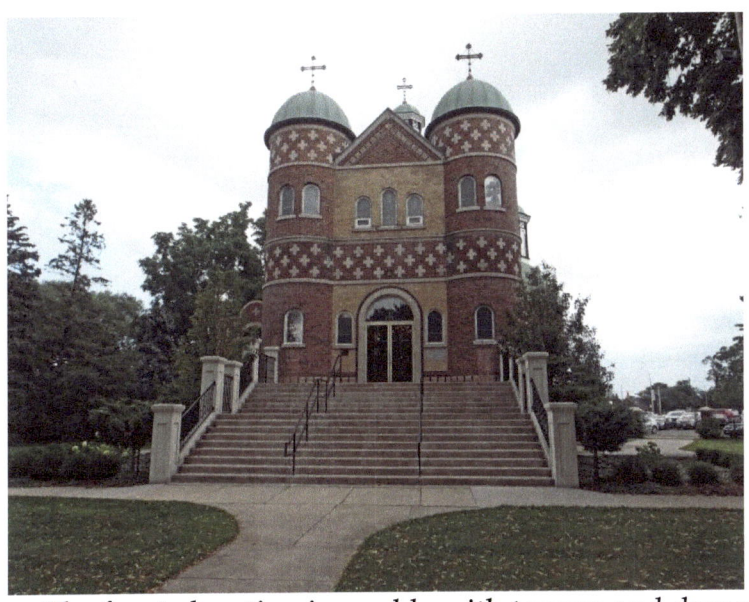

The front elevation is a gable with towers and domes symmetrically placed on either side. The front entrance features a grand tiled staircase with decorative pre-cast concrete piers and painted iron railings. The glass doors and semi-circular transom above are trimmed with stone. The windows are semi-circular and trimmed with brick or stone.

Architectural Terms

Agraffe: A decorative central keystone in an arch, often carved with a human face, cartouche or floral design. Example: 169 St. Paul Crescent, Page 36	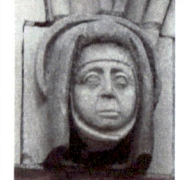
Balustrade: A railing system, generally around a balcony or on a second level, consisting of balusters and a top rail Example: 22 Bayview Drive, Page 9	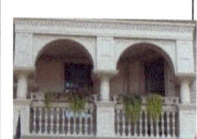
Bay Window: A window that projects out from a wall, in a semicircular, rectangular, or polygonal design. Used frequently in Gothic and Victorian designs. Example: 52 Bayview Drive, Page 13	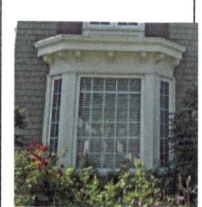
Brackets: a decorative or weight-bearing structural element which forms a right angle with one side against a wall and the other under a projecting surface such as an eave or roof. Example: 343 Merritt Street, Page 44	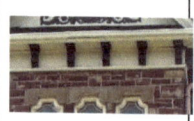
Buttress: a masonry structure built against or projecting from a wall which serves to support or reinforce the wall. In Canadian architecture, they are sometimes used for decoration. Example: 169 St Paul Crescent, Page 36	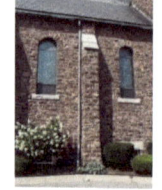

Capital: The uppermost finish or decoration on a column. A Doric column is characterized by a plain column with no base, a shaft with twenty flutings, and a simple capital with a simple entablature. Example: 20 Bayview Drive, Page 8	
Course: continuous horizontal row or layer of stone or brick. Example: 343 Merritt Street, Page 44	
Cupola: A domed or curved roof rising from a building as a decorative element. Example: Bayview Drive, Page 23	
Dentil Moulding: an even series of rectangles used as ornamental decoration in cornices. Example: 22 Bayview Drive, Page 9	
Dichromatic brickwork: the use of two colours of brick, tile or slate to decorate a façade. Example: 337-341 Merritt Street, Page 42	

Dome: Any roof structure that is curved and spans an ultimately circular base. Squinches and pendentives are used to provide a circular base on a square or rectilinear tower. A squinch is a construction filling in the upper angles of a square room so as to form a base to receive an octagonal **or** spherical dome. When a square space is vaulted to provide a circular space for a dome the resulting curved triangular supports are called pendentives. This is most common in Byzantine architecture. Example: 124 Rolls Avenue, Page 50	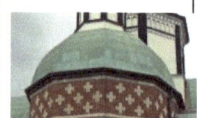
Dormer: (French for "sleep") a gable end window that pierces through the plane of a sloping roof surface to create usable space in the top floor or attic of a building by adding headroom. Example: Bayview Drive, Page 23	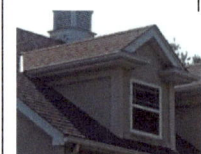
Entrance: The entrance encompasses the doorway and the inner vestibule or, in residential architecture, the covered porch. Example: 22 Bayview Drive, Page 9	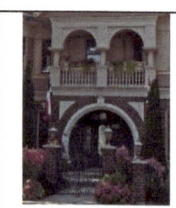
Gable: the triangular portion of a wall between the edges of a sloping roof. Example: Bayview Drive, Page 10	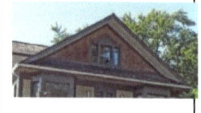

Gambrel Roof: a symmetrical two-sided roof with two slopes on each side; the upper slope is positioned at a shallow angle, while the lower slope is steep. It is similar to a mansard roof, but a gambrel has vertical gable ends instead of being hipped at the four corners of the building. Example: Johnston Street, Page 29	
Hipped Roof: a roof where all sides slope downwards to the walls with no gables. Example: 9 Johnston Street, Page 30	
Iron Cresting: A decorative ornament along the top of a roof. Iron cresting was popular in the Baroque era and also in Italianate, Victorian, Second Empire and Queen Anne styles of architecture. Example: 56 Bayview Drive, Page 14	
Keystones and Voussoirs: a voussoir is a wedge-shaped element used in building an arch. A keystone is the central stone that locks all the stones into position, allowing the arch to bear weight. A keystone is often enlarged and embellished. Example: 337-341 Merritt Street, Page 42	
Lancet Window: a tall, narrow window with a pointed arch at its top. Example: 372 Merritt Street, Page 45	

Mansard Roof: This style was popularized by Francois Mansart (1598-1666), an accomplished architect of the French Baroque period and especially fashionable during the Second French Empire (1852-1870). This roof is almost flat on the top section, with two slopes on each of its sides with the lower slope at a steeper angle than the upper, and has dormer windows. Example: 18 Bayview Drive, Page 7	
Palladian Window: a large window that is divided into three sections with the centre section larger than the two side sections and usually arched. Example: Johnston Street, Page 32	
Parapet: low wall around the edge of a roof. Example: 344 Merritt Street, Page 43	
Pediment: a triangular section above the door or portico, usually supported by columns. The inside of the triangle is called the tympanum. Example: Johnston Street, Page 31	
Quoin: masonry blocks at the corner of a wall, often a decorative feature, usually larger or of a different colour than the rest of the wall. Example: 135 Bradley Street, Page 38	
Rose Window: a circular window with ornamental tracery radiating from the centre. Example: 169 St Paul Crescent, Page 36	

Sidelight: a vertical window that flanks a door, and is often used to emphasize the importance of a primary entrance. **Transom Window:** the light above the doorway, also called a fanlight. Example: 18 Johnston Street, Page 30	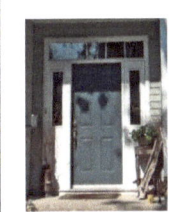
Tower: A circular, square, or octagonal vertical structure higher than the surrounding structure that is usually part of an existing building and is created either for extra defense or for a specific purpose such as a clock or a bell tower. Example: 372 Merritt Street, Page 45	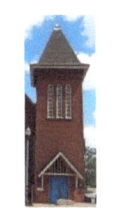
Turret: a small tower that projects from the wall of a building. Example: 22 Bayview Drive, Page 9	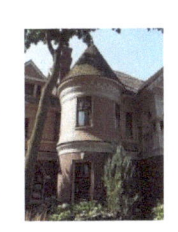
Verge board and Finial: also called bargeboards – hang from the projecting end of a roof and are often elaborately carved and ornamented. **Finial:** ornament added to the top of a gable, pinnacle, canopy or spire – a Gothic element. Example: 35 Johnston Street, Page 34	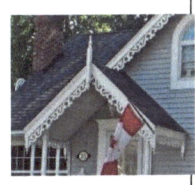

Building Styles

Byzantine Revival (or **Neo-Byzantine**) 1840s-1870s: was most frequently seen in religious, institutional and public buildings. Neo-Byzantine architecture incorporates elements of the Byzantine style associated with Eastern and Orthodox Christian architecture dating from the 5th through 11th centuries. The character of Byzantine architecture is determined by the development of the dome to cover polygonal and square plans for churches, tombs, and baptisteries. The practice of placing many domes over one building is in strong contrast to the Romanesque system of vaulted roofs. The system of construction in concrete and brickwork introduced by the Romans was adopted by the Byzantines. The skeleton of concrete and brickwork was first completed and allowed to settle before the surface sheathing of unyielding marble slabs was added. Brickwork lent itself externally to decorative whimsy in patterns and banding, and internally it was suitable for covering with marble, mosaic and fresco decoration. The grouping of small domes or semi-domes round the large central dome was one of the most remarkable peculiarities of Byzantine churches; the exterior closely corresponds with the interior. The features of the style are multiple domes, round-arched windows, and ample decoration.
Example: 124 Rolls Avenue, Page 50

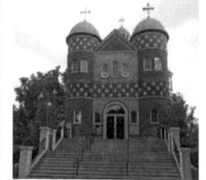

Neo-colonial (also Colonial Revival, Georgian Revival or Neo-Georgian) architecture seeks to revive elements of architectural style of American colonial architecture of the period around the Revolutionary War which drew strongly from Georgian architecture of Great Britain. Architecture from the 18th and early 19th centuries in Ontario includes a wide assortment of detailing and ornament applied to a design centered around the fireplace and the source of water. Structures are typically two stories, have a symmetrical front facade with elaborate front doorways, often with decorative crown pediments, fanlights, and sidelights, symmetrical windows flanking the front entrance, often in pairs or threes, and columned porches. Example: Johnston Street, Page 29	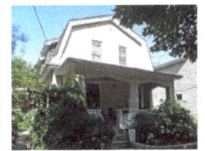
Regency Cottage, 1830-1860 – This style originated in England in 1815 and spread to Ontario later in the 19th century as British officers retired to Canada. It is a modest one-storey house with a low-pitched hip roof and has a symmetrical front façade. Example: 31 Bayview Drive, Page 10	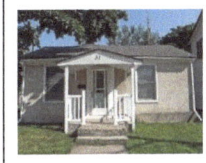

Romanesque Revival, 1880-1910 – This style hearkens back to medieval architecture of the 11th and 12th centuries with a heavy appearance, blocky towers and rounded arches. Example: 169 St. Paul Crescent, Page 36	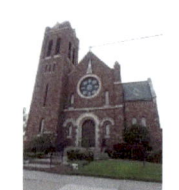
Tudor Revival – exposed timbers with stucco infill, multi-paned windows. Example: 56 Bayview Drive, Page 14	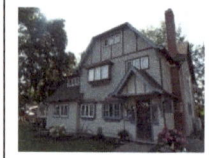
Victorian - In Ontario, a Victorian style building can be seen as any building built between 1840 and 1900 that doesn't fit into any of the other categories. It encompasses a large group of buildings constructed in brick, stone, and timber, using an eclectic mixture of Classical and Gothic motifs. Example: 343 Merritt Street, Page 44	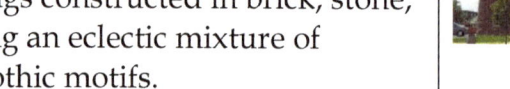

www.ingramcontent.com/pod-product-compliance
Lightning Source LLC
Chambersburg PA
CBHW040238220526

45473CB00001B/285